How to Study

A practical guide from a Christian perspective

Edward J. Shewan

Christian Liberty Press
Arlington Heights, Illinois

A publication of

Christian Liberty Press

502 West Euclid Avenue
Arlington Heights, Illinois 60004
www.christianlibertypress.com

Copyediting by Diane C. Olson
Layout by Edward J. Shewan
Cover design by Bob Fine
Cover image by Darren Greenwood, copyright © DesignPics, Inc.

ISBN 978-1-932971-34-7
1-932971-34-3

All Scripture references are from the *Holy Bible*, King James Version, unless otherwise indicated.

Printed in the United States of America

TO THE TEACHER

Each student has different needs, abilities, and problems to be addressed. Therefore, the parent or instructor should guide the student by using the following steps:

(1) determine the student's level of skills,

(2) identify areas of difficulty, and

(3) coach the student accordingly.

As the student practices under supervision, the parent can build motivation and help transfer the skills the student has learned to actual course work. Each student should realize the importance of these rules and procedures and believe that pursuing them is worthwhile.

About the Author

Edward Shewan is Managing Editor for Christian Liberty Press. He graduated from Valparaiso University in 1974. After a year of mission work in Africa, he attended the Moody Bible Institute's Advanced Studies Program in 1976. Subsequently, he served in Chicago city churches for ten years. In 1983 he graduated from Trinity Evangelical Divinity School with an M.Div. degree. He has served over fifteen years as a writer and editor for Christian Liberty Press. Edward, his wife Belit, and three daughters live in Streamwood, Illinois, and attend Grace Community Bible Church, a Reformed congregation in Roselle, Illinois.

This book is dedicated to my parents:

Dr. William Shewan
and
Marjorie Ruth Shewan

PREFACE

This guide meets a real need for those who desire to improve their reading, writing, and studying skills. *How to Study* simply and clearly explains how you can learn the craft of studying. Studying can be considered a craft because it requires a special type of work. As the Apostle Paul exhorts Timothy, "Study to shew thyself approved unto God, a workman that needeth not to be ashamed" (2 Timothy 2:15). Each student needs to apply his or her mind—exerting energy to acquire knowledge and understanding of God's creation. Such a workman seeks to please God and will not be ashamed when his work is brought into judgment.

> *And further, by these, my son, be admonished: of making many books there is no end; and much study is a weariness of the flesh. Let us hear the conclusion of the whole matter: Fear God, and keep his commandments: for this is the whole duty of man. For God shall bring every work into judgment, with every secret thing, whether it be good, or whether it be evil.*
> *Ecclesiastes 12:12–14*

Most subjects in the curriculum are addressed in *How to Study*, and basic skills have been selected accordingly. These skills are easily transferable, so you can readily use them in your studies. There are no short cuts to the learning process, but many time-saving steps have been presented to help you acquire the information you desire. These rules and procedures are explained in a concise manner, and the illustrations show exactly how to use them. Confidence and success in your studies will be achieved as you seek to please God and apply these skills.

TABLE OF CONTENTS

LET'S GET STARTED

How *do* you study? In an overstuffed chair with your iPod™ blaring? Slouched on the couch in front of the television, with a sandwich in one hand and a book in the other? Some people can study almost anywhere and under any condition. But if we want to please God and do our best, all of us must honestly look at where and how we study. A quiet spot is the ideal. We learn in the Psalms that David often meditated on God's Word in the quiet hours of the night. In fact, Psalm 119:99 declares that a person will have "more understanding than all [his] teachers" if he quietly reflects upon God's testimonies. Quietness helps us not only in studying God's Word, but also in all areas of learning.

Many teachers have recommended guidelines to follow for those who want to study under the proper conditions. These have been summarized as follows:

1. **Use adequate lighting** when studying. If the lighting is poor, your eyes will become strained and tired.
2. **Follow a set schedule.** Develop the habit of studying at the same time each day—when you are most alert.
3. **Study in a quiet spot**, free from anyone or anything that might distract your concentration. A quiet spirit is also an immense asset.
4. **Obtain all your supplies** (pen, paper, text, ruler, notebook, and so forth), before you begin studying. In this way you will not waste time and energy.
5. **Use a table or desk as a work station**, and obtain a comfortable chair. Sitting up straight with your feet on the floor helps to keep you alert.
6. **Keep track of your assignments** in a notebook or a weekly chart. Assignments should be marked off as you complete each one of them.
7. **Plan to work for a whole block of time**, without interruption. You will usually finish in less time than allotted.
8. **Do any written work right away.** Start out with a rough draft. Correct any mistakes, and then rewrite the final copy.
9. **Study with a goal in mind.** Why are you reading a given section or chapter? Take notes and do not get sidetracked.
10. **Schedule free time each day** for reading a passage from the Bible, a particular article, or a favorite book to revitalize your heart and mind.

1. STUDY TO SHOW THYSELF APPROVED

Too often we approach most tasks without consulting the Lord or His Word. Either we are smug in our understanding of what we think the Bible says on any given topic, or worse yet, we are altogether complacent towards the things of Christ. However, the Apostle Paul—who is like a father to Timothy—exhorts him to take everything that he has told him and "the same commit thou to faithful men, who shall be able to teach others also" (2 Timothy 2:2). Because Timothy was faithful and passed on what he learned from his spiritual father to other faithful men, the message of God's grace and forgiveness has come down to us through the ages, 2,000 years later.

But Paul does not stop there. He further encourages Timothy to "**Study to shew thyself approved unto God**, a workman that needeth not to be ashamed, rightly dividing the word of truth" (2 Timothy 2:15). Paul expected Timothy to spread this "word of truth" to the ends of the earth, but not without *studying* first. Obviously this refers to studying God's Word and "rightly dividing the word of truth." We too have been called of God, and sent by Christ to "teach all nations … to observe all things whatsoever I have commanded you …" (Matthew 28:19, 20). As disciples of Christ we must hear and obey all that He has told us to do, just like Timothy received the truth concerning Christ and committed it to other faithful men.

Therefore, as Christians and as students, we should seek to know and understand God's will in all that we say and do—even when we study. Each of us should seek to learn all we can regarding God's Word and His world. The course work, which has been especially developed for you according to your abilities, has incorporated those subjects that will help you grow in your knowledge of the Bible and His creation. So, take advantage of this God-ordained time in your life to study—and study with all your heart, soul, mind, and strength (Mark 12:30). Your love and devotion towards the Lord Jesus will be reflected in your words and actions—and by the way you study.

Another important aspect of approaching your studies from a Christian perspective is the **spiritual warfare** that you face now and will face in the future. The Apostle Paul reminds the believers in Ephesus that "we wrestle not against flesh and blood, but against principalities, against powers, against rulers of the darkness of this world, against spiritual wickedness in high places. Wherefore take unto you the whole armour of God, that ye may be able to withstand in the evil day, and having done all, to stand" (Ephesians 6:12–13). Therefore, we must know God's Word—"the *sword of the Spirit*, which is the word of God" (v. 17)—and be able to use it. "For the word of God is quick, and powerful, and sharper than any *twoedged sword*, piercing even to the dividing asunder of soul and spirit, and of the joints and marrow, and is a discerner of the thoughts and intents of the heart" (Hebrews 4:12).

How do your thoughts measure up? What are the intentions of your heart? You must "… present your bodies a living sacrifice, holy, acceptable unto God, which is your reasonable service. And be not conformed to this world: but be ye *transformed by the renewing of your mind*, that ye may prove what is that good, and acceptable, and perfect, will of God" (Romans 12:1–2). Our minds need to be cleansed "with the washing of water by the word" (Ephesians 5: 26), so we will be able to discern between good and evil. As you learn, you should get in the habit of holding all that you read and study up to the "mirror" of God's Word—"But whoso looketh into *the perfect law of liberty*, and continueth therein, he being not a forgetful hearer, but a doer of the work, this man shall be blessed in his deed" (James 1:25).

As you progress in your studies and in life, you will be exposed to all kinds of teachings and ideas. Therefore, you must be ready in and out of season, "For the time will come when they will not endure *sound doctrine*; but after their own lusts shall they heap to themselves teachers, having itching ears; And they shall turn away their ears from the truth, and shall be turned unto fables" (2 Timothy 4:3–4). Especially if you plan to go on to college, you must be well-grounded in the Word: "That we henceforth be no more children, tossed to and fro, and carried about with every wind of doctrine, by the sleight of men, and cunning craftiness, whereby they lie in wait to deceive" (Ephesians 4:14). So instead of being swayed by the clever eloquence of men, you will "know how ye ought to answer every man" (Colossians 4:6).

Study to show yourself approved unto God, a workman that does not need to be ashamed of your age or status in life. But as God gives you grace, rightly handle God's truth so you will know right from wrong, good from evil, and the truth from Satan's lies. And as you study, make it a goal to study the powerful, life-changing Word of God. May it be your guide and defender in all that you think, say, and do!

O LORD, make me know my end and what is the measure of my days; let me know how fleeting I am! Behold, you have made my days a few handbreadths, and my lifetime is as nothing before you. Surely all mankind stands as a mere breath!

Psalm 39:4-5 (ESV)

As each has received a gift, use it to serve one another, as good stewards of God's varied grace.

1 Peter 4:10 (ESV)

2. REDEEMING THE TIME

Time management is a key factor for anyone who seeks to improve in the area of study habits. In fact, handling time properly is half the battle. The Bible says, "See then that ye walk circumspectly, not as fools, but as wise, *redeeming the time*, because the days are evil" (Ephesians 5:15, 16). Everyone has the same twenty-four hours to complete the tasks at hand, but not everyone uses these hours wisely.

Each student can redeem the time by keeping a *time diary*. A simple chart makes the best time diary, where weekdays are placed across the top of the chart, and all the activities of the day are listed down the left-hand column. Such activities as devotions, sleeping, eating, studying, working, exercising, and socializing are some that may be enumerated. Enter the estimated time you would normally spend doing each activity in the appropriate box. Sunday should always be allocated as a day of worship and rest (see Genesis 2:2-3, Hebrews 10:25). Out of the 144 hours (or 6 days) we have left, let's say 48 hours are set aside for sleeping, 16 hours for eating, and 30 hours for an outside job and some kind of recreation. This would leave approximately seven to eight hours per day for classes and studying. Examine the suggested *time diary* below:

	Sun	Mon	Tues	Wed	Thur	Fri	Sat
Devotions							
Sleeping							
Eating							
Class Time	- 0 -						
Studying	- 0 -						
Working	- 0 -						
Exercising	- 0 -						
Socializing	- 0 -						

Figure 0.1 Time Diary

4

How do you spend your week? Make an honest evaluation of how you have been using your every waking hour. And then chart a new time diary that would reflect your desire to redeem the time God has given each of us to manage.

3. Long-term Scheduling

The first thing you need to create is your *long-term schedule*, a single-page calendar listing each month with spaces to fill in self-imposed deadlines for tests, daily work, special projects, and book reports. Researching and writing a paper takes quite a bit of time; therefore, this should be broken down into a step-by-step approach over a longer period of time. You will not be able to remember everything you need to do; consequently, you should schedule all your known assignments. In this way, you will be able to do each task one day at a time.

Your overall course work will not intimidate you, if you spread it out and tackle it bit by bit. Study by a planned schedule, which saves time and effort. This approach is more efficient and most rewarding. Without a schedule, you will find yourself paralyzed by indecision: "What should I do first? Should I spend one hour or two on this assignment? Am I going to finish that project on time?" Your goal should be to make studying not only a habit, but spontaneous as well. Do not be distracted by the tyranny of the urgent. By sticking to the plan, you will escape the frustration and guilt for not doing your best on your assignments. Give each task adequate attention. Plan ahead!

JAN	FEB	MAR	APR

MAY	JUNE	JULY	AUG

SEPT	OCT	NOV	DEC

Figure 0.2 Long-term Schedule

4. SHORT-TERM SCHEDULING

A *weekly schedule* is a must. Create your own schedule, including each of your class assignments, on a daily basis. You may want to use a spreadsheet program like Excel® for this purpose. A one-page schedule should be set up with the *days of the week* across the top, and the *hours of the day* from 6:00 a.m. to  11:00 p.m. listed along the left-hand column (see page 7). Once you have completed your schedule, you could even have it enlarged to add needed information. However, do not let your schedule control your life. Be flexible enough to make adjustments as you go. You should schedule the following activities:

- Morning Bible study
- Scripture memory
- Prayer
- Class/study times
- Meals
- Recreation
- Social/sports events
- Job hours
- Library time
- Sunday worship
- Ministering to others
- Group Bible study
- Free time

Figure 0.3 Daily Activities

Scheduling each hour of the day will give you much more free time than you ever expected. And, do not forget that *Saturday is a workday*. We are to labor six days; so you should study, do household tasks, or get a job on this day. Finally, Sunday is a day for worshiping our Lord Jesus—resting our souls and bodies, as well as fellowshipping with other Christians. Sunday is *not* a time for studying. There is always the temptation to use this day for work or study. However, commit yourself to keeping the Lord's Day holy. Give your heart, soul, mind, and body one day to rest during the week. It will work wonders.

Time	Sun	Mon	Tues	Wed	Thur	Fri	Sat
6:00 am							
7:00							
8:00							
9:00							
*							
*							
*							
8:00 pm							
9:00							
10:00							
11:00							

Figure 0.4 Weekly Schedule

Helpful Hints

Here are some helpful hints to follow for *redeeming the time*:

1. **Place your long-term schedule prominently.** If you have a set work station, put this schedule on the wall or on your desk in front of you. Check your long-term schedule periodically because you do not want any surprises.

2. **Consult your short-term schedule often.** Plan to study the same thing at the same time each day. Establishing regular study habits will help you avoid procrastination. Check your weekly, short-term schedule daily.

3. **Structure your schedule with your *needs* and *gifts* in mind.** Some assignments on your schedule may cause you great anxiety, but they still need to be done. Others may come easily, and you will be tempted to do them first. Therefore, make your schedule balanced; otherwise, you will never seem able to tackle your more troublesome subjects. The best approach is to *study the more difficult assignments first*.

4. **Be flexible.** Design your schedule to meet the unexpected. If your plan is flexible, it will be easier to keep yourself motivated. Do not be caught by surprise. *Anticipate the unforeseen, and reschedule.* However, do not fall into the trap of rationalizing everything that comes along.

5. **Find the best spot in your room to study**, but not on the bed. A *well-lighted desk* is the best place to study, including all your basic study materials close at hand. Having a set location to study goes a long way toward improving your study habits and redeeming the time.

6. **A small library of reference books** should be on your desk, including a *dictionary* and *thesaurus*, and any other books you deem helpful. And without a doubt, do not forget the most important book of all—your ***Bible***.

7. **Avoid any and all distractions.** By all means, turn off any electronic media. Silence *is* golden. Also, do not waste time by answering the phone every time it rings.

I said in mine heart, God shall judge the righteous and the wicked: for there is a time there for every purpose and for every work.
Ecclesiastes 3:17

CHAPTER ONE

IMPROVING
YOUR READING APTITUDE

The most important single factor of your entire education may be developing a *habit of reading*. A love for reading is something that is more easily caught than taught; therefore, seek to nurture such a habit by opening your mind's eye to the marvelous world of literature, yet to be discovered. You will be able to go places you never dreamed possible and learn things once beyond your grasp. So begin the adventure with books you enjoy. A knowledge of words and a taste for books are two of life's enduring treasures. They will become your never failing companions. If you are one of the fortunate ones who has acquired a passion for reading, you are perhaps one of the happiest people in the world.

1. THE WONDER OF WORDS

Language is our vehicle of thought, the means by which we formulate all our ideas in terms of *words*—both spoken and written. If we restrict our thinking and learning only to the words we hear or speak, the development of our intellect will be very limited. However, the written word offers a great depository for all our complex thought processes. Each one of us should be able to access this wonderful world of words, and in so doing we will be able to grow and develop our mental capabilities.

The term "language" is derived from the word *lingua*, which in Latin means "tongue." Therefore, the sounds and utterances that are made with the tongue are ideas in terms of spoken words. They express the internal dialogue within each and every human being. These spoken words are transcribed into sound-symbols on paper. In addition, as you read written words, they are then translated back into spoken words. Consequently, a word consists of a sound or series of sounds used to verbally communicate meaning, and is represented by a letter or group of letters when written.

Therefore, the ability to read consists of translating written words accurately back into their spoken counterparts. Likewise, the ability to write consists of transcribing spoken words into written sound-symbols. The *alphabet* provides us with the set of symbols or letters needed to accomplish this two-way process. We use twenty-six letters to represent about forty-four speech sounds in our alphabet. However, the problem with the English writing system is the limited sounds that the symbols represent. Furthermore, English has been enriched by the invasion of other languages; thus our writing system has a large number of irregularities and inconsistencies. But once these have been mastered, there are few problems in learning to read and write these words.

2. THE DIDACTIC DICTIONARY

Access to the wonderful world of words begins with an amazing book that should become one of your life-long friends, if it is not already. This book is the ***dictionary***. Books, newspapers, and magazines are filled with new and strange words that express writers' thoughts. The dictionary can be a useful guide to help you understand these new words. An excellent habit you can develop is to instantly use the dictionary every time you see or hear a new word—fixing its correct pronunciation and exact meaning clearly in your mind.

Another rewarding discipline is to discover from where a word comes. This is called learning the *etymology* of a word, or tracing a term back as far as possible in its own language—to its source in contemporary or earlier languages. Insights into the current usage of a word can be gained from a full knowledge of the word's history. In fact, a better understanding of language, in general, can be achieved from knowing how words are related to other terms in the English language or other Indo-European languages. Etymologies normally appear in dictionaries following the *part-of-speech* label and are usually inside brackets of some sort—clearly distinguishing them from the proper definitions. Various symbols are used in identifying language sources, and a list of these symbols normally appears at the front of the dictionary.

Obviously, to locate a word in the dictionary, you need to use the **guide words** at the top of the page. The guide word on the left side of the page indicates the first word or first complete entry on that page; the one on the right side refers to the last entry on the page. Once the word is found, the spelling should be checked, the pronunciation must be learned, and the part-of-speech needs to be verified. Finally, you should examine the one or more given definitions to determine the exact meaning that best fits the word as it is used in the sentence.

The following steps show you how to use the dictionary:

1.   Learn the exact **pronunciation** of each word. A word is frequently respelled to help the reader enunciate it correctly: *hed* for *head*.

2.   Certain letters are marked to explain how they should be pronounced. A **pronunciation key**, usually found at the bottom of the right-hand pages, tells what sounds the marks stand for.

3.   Each word is divided into **syllables**, which are separated by a small space or a dot. An **accent mark** (′) shows which syllable(s) should be emphasized when the word is being pronounced.

4.   Check the **spelling** of the word. Sometimes there are two spellings given for a word. The first spelling is usually the one that is preferred: *adviser* or *advisor*; *enroll* or *enrol*.

5.   Verify the **part-of-speech** of the word. This is particularly helpful with verbs, adverbs, and adjectives. The part-of-speech is usually indicated by an italicized letter(s) after the pronunciation of the word: *vt*. signifies a transitive verb.

6.   Examine the **etymology** of the word. This is usually located in boldface brackets following the part-of-speech. This will give valuable insights into the current usage of a word and a better understanding of our language overall: the word ***Bible*** is derived from the Greek word for "book," and ultimately comes from the ancient Phoenician city of *Byblos*—the port from which papyrus (*biblos*) was exported.

7.   Choose the **meaning** that best fits the way a word is used in the sentence. The word *crop*, for example, may mean a short haircut, a riding whip, a swollen saclike gullet of a bird, or any agricultural product.

3. A Voluminous Vocabulary

A good author, poet, lyricist, or orator works hard to express his or her ideas clearly and forcefully. The desired effect is to instantly capture the interest of the reader or listener. Such people hope to make others understand and act upon what has been communicated. By reading good books and using a good dictionary on a regular basis, you too will be able to express your ideas with ease. The dictionary holds a wealth of information about many powerful, vivid words; therefore, it should not be neglected as you develop your ***vocabulary***.

In fact, every word that you use is important. For example, have you ever noticed how significant a simple greeting can be? Just two words like "Good morning" can make someone's day. Of course, the way you say it reflects your attitude or feelings toward the person you are addressing. But carefully chosen words, as well as one's tone of voice and facial expressions, are valuable tools in effective communication.

Here are ten rules for improving one's vocabulary:

1. **Examine each new word carefully.** Do this on a regular basis in all your subjects. Then incorporate the word into your vocabulary.

2. **Make a list of all the new words you** *read* as you study, especially in science and history. Every few weeks, review these words until they become familiar to you.

3. **Keep a list of all the new words you** *hear* others use. Look them up in the dictionary and regularly review them.

4. **Discover the meaning** of each new word from the context of the sentence it appears in, especially when your dictionary is not available.

5. **Explore the various meanings** an ordinary word may possess. Do you know the different meanings of these words? *crop, sponge, frank*

6. **Search through its word-family.** A word-family refers to all the terms that can be extracted from the **root** of a word: *image* (imagery, imaginable, imaginary, imagination, imaginative, imagine). Try these roots: *value, save, prefer*

7. **Analyze the roots, prefixes, or suffixes** of the word. Examine each of the following words: *preview, helpless, independent*

8. **Learn to break every word into syllables**, and pay attention to which syllables are emphasized. Study how these words are divided into syllables and emphasized: *pre/**dom**/i/nate, ex/**tem**/po/ra/ne/ous, cen/**trif**/u/gal.*

9. **Use your dictionary on a daily basis.** When you are not sure of the meaning that a new word holds, look it up immediately: *egregious–remarkably bad.*

10. **Put your new word(s) to work** as soon as possible. Make each new word a part of your speech and writing. Try to use them correctly the same day: *The **egregious** man lied and cheated.*

Vocabulary Test

The words in **boldface** below are ninth grade level terms, which are followed by a list of four possible one-word definitions. Photocopy this page, then take the test—see how many of these words you know by underlining the one that best fits the meaning of the **boldface** word. Upon completing the test, look up the exact meaning of each word in your dictionary. If you have missed three or more, you should spend time on improving your vocabulary skills. The first one is done for you as an example:

1.	**genuine**	sharp	<u>real</u>	false	gold
2.	**shrewd**	smart	cunning	superb	jealous
3.	**frighten**	scare	awful	deceive	frigid
4.	**stubborn**	obstinate	flexible	studious	forceful
5.	**imitate**	begin	copy	prepare	imply
6.	**conscious**	surrender	prepare	honest	aware
7.	**recollect**	remember	refer	gathering	purpose
8.	**ingenuity**	skillful	creativity	honest	clever
9.	**vigorously**	expressly	powerfully	swiftly	clearly
10.	**amend**	vote	refer to	change	recall
11.	**arduous**	courageous	difficult	forceful	comply
12.	**epoch**	age	concentrate	poem	plan
13.	**fortitude**	fortunate	courage	many	avarice
14.	**admonish**	reward	prepare	warn	belittle
15.	**charred**	painted	wood	burned	recalled
16.	**remote**	remiss	distant	repose	redeem
17.	**tranquil**	helpful	peaceful	excited	transfer
18.	**obsolete**	created	out of date	different	futile
19.	**vestige**	clothing	laughing	special	trace
20.	**evade**	attempt	refuse	avoid	attack
21.	**thwart**	permit	present	throw	hinder
22.	**censure**	criticize	cement	praise	dishonor
23.	**designate**	proclaim	appoint	prepare	aimless
24.	**accelerate**	speed up	continue	emphasize	space
25.	**precision**	artistic	exactness	malicious	crude

4. SUPER SPELLER

To become a *good speller* takes discipline. Since most of your course work demands it, then being the best speller possible is a commendable goal. From now on your efforts will be judged in part on how well you can spell. If you follow the basic steps outlined here, and learn how to spell even the most difficult words you come across, your overall chances to succeed will improve. Also, beware of certain subjects that have special words that should be studied on an individual basis—scientific concepts, biological terms, and names of mathematical formulas. In addition to this, whatever papers you hand in or exams you take will be assessed, in some way, on how well you spell. This will either help or hinder your best efforts. Study the next **five rules**, so you can work towards becoming a "super speller":

Rule #1   **Pronounce the word properly.** If you do not know its pronunciation, look it up in your dictionary for the correct way. Reinforce the meaning of the word by using it in a sentence.

Rule #2   **Repeat the word by syllables.** Your dictionary will also help you in dividing the word with the proper voicing, inflection, and emphasis.

Rule #3   **Try to spell it from memory.** If you have any trouble, look at it again. Pronounce each syllable correctly. Then spell it without looking.

Rule #4   **Write the word accurately** on a three-by-five card. Make note of any particular letter or combination of letters that are not pronounced.

Rule #5   **Spell the word correctly.** Write the word down again; pronounce each syllable clearly; and try to spell it. If you can do this, you are well on your way to becoming a good speller.

Listed below are more than 100 of the most misspelled words by the average student. Go through this list to find out how many you can spell properly. If you have any problems, immediately begin to master them. At your convenience, make a set of index cards with these words or any others that you may find. Use the **five rules** above to help you conquer them—one by one. Occasionally review the words on your list, and work toward becoming a "super speller."

I'll	I'm	October	summer	write	him
Mrs.	want	tomorrow	because	address	now
are	them	handkerchief	cousin	already	here
you	that's	Christmas	balloon	didn't	ever
am	your	Halloween	brought	should	play
arm	from	together	haven't	every	they
how	right	teacher's	you're	science	like
will	were	morning	writing	friend	just
two	name	Thanksgiving	where	would	then
too	when	swimming	good-by	today	sure

hour	down	stationary	receive	school	time
our	some	all right	o'clock	while	very
went	don't	sometimes	suppose	going	until
to	there	Saturday	separate	won't	their
one	letter	everybody	mother	tonight	little
its	know	birthday	getting	coming	with
was	guess	February	pretty	Sunday	have

Becoming a perfect speller takes effort, so keep your dictionary close by to check any new or difficult words that might come up. Your reading and studying will be enhanced as you become familiar with more and more new words. In addition, as you learn good spelling skills, you will benefit by being able to read more quickly and understand more. Moreover, when you write a theme, an essay, or term paper, you will also be able to expand your vocabulary, produce better work, and excel on your exams.

5. READY TO READ

One of the most striking ways to improve your reading comprehension is to read **phrase-by-phrase**. Many trudge along word-by-word, but you will be amazed how your understanding will make an about face when you use this technique. Your eyes will adjust to *thought groups*, rather than focusing on mere words. In a short period of time, your speed will not only escalate, but your comprehension will increase. Start with three or four words at a time, then increase the number of words to five or six. In no time, you will be astonished at both your speed and comprehension.

Here are ten questions that will help you improve your reading aptitude:

1. **Why are you reading?** At the outset *establish a reading goal.* Determine why you are reading: either for pleasure, information, lesson preparation, historical background, or research purposes.
2. **Do you remember what you read?** Try to make it your *aim to recall* what you are reading. Practice reading for comprehension's sake only.
3. **Do you read word-by-word?** One of the most effective ways to boost your understanding is to read *phrase-by-phrase.* Initially, try three or four words at a time; then try five or six.
4. **Do you look for words?** *Words* are important, but focusing in on *ideas* guides you through the author's thoughts and helps your comprehension.

5. **Do you summarize each paragraph?** Quickly try to *grasp the key idea* of the paragraph. This will help you understand the flow of the author's argument, reinforcing his overall purpose.
6. **How fast do you read?** Try to *increase your rate of reading* by timing yourself. Read a given segment, count the words you read, and divide by the length of time it took to read it. This will give you the rate at which you read. Reading *phrase-by-phrase* will improve your speed.
7. **Do you ever catch yourself reading without thinking?** Your lips are moving, but your mind is not engaged. You end up going back over the same material time and time again. Make sure you *focus on the matter at hand*, so time will not be wasted.
8. **Do you daydream?** *Learn to concentrate* and do not be easily distracted by your surroundings. Do not let an idea that you have read get you sidetracked, either. Stick with the task at hand.
9. **Do you reinforce what you have read?** The best way to keep up on what you are reading is to ask yourself questions that will *fortify the key ideas* and keep your overall perspective.
10. **Do you read with your fingertips?** It is of essence that you develop the habit of *reading with your eyes*, not with your fingertips. In this respect, the hand is *not* quicker than the eye.

Try reading the two following portions using the skills you have learned in this section:

The Twenty-third Psalm

A Psalm of David

The LORD is my shepherd; / I shall not want. / He maketh me to lie down in green pastures: / he leadeth me beside the still waters. / He restoreth my soul: / he leadeth me in the paths of righteousness / for his name's sake. / Yea, though I walk through the valley of the shadow of death, / I will fear no evil: / for thou art with me; / thy rod and thy staff they comfort me. / Thou preparest a table before me in the presence of mine enemies: / thou anointest my head with oil; / my cup runneth over. / Surely goodness and mercy shall follow me all the days of my life: / and I will dwell in the house of the LORD for ever.

Reading time: 20 seconds

Before you begin the following reading, try to understand the setting—the time of civil strife and the place where so many had lost their lives—and the circumstances surrounding the event that prompted President Lincoln to deliver this address.

Gettysburg Address

by Abraham Lincoln

Fourscore and seven years ago / our fathers brought forth on this continent, / a new nation, / conceived in liberty, and dedicated to the proposition / that all men are created equal.

Now we are engaged in a great civil war, / testing whether that nation, / or any nation / so conceived and so dedicated, / can long endure. / We are met on a great battlefield of that war. / We have come to dedicate a portion of that field / as a final resting place for those who here gave their lives / that that nation might live. / It is altogether fitting and proper that we should do this.

But, in a larger sense, we cannot dedicate ... we cannot consecrate ... we cannot hallow ... this ground. / The brave men, living and dead, who struggled here, / have consecrated it far above our poor power to add or detract. / The world will little note / nor long remember what we say here, / but it can never forget what they did here. / It is for us, the living, / rather, to be dedicated here to the unfinished work / which they who fought here have thus far so nobly advanced. / It is rather for us to be here dedicated to the great task remaining before us ... that from these honored dead we take increased devotion / to that cause for which they gave the last full measure of devotion; that we here highly resolve / that these dead shall not have died in vain; / that this nation, under God, shall have a new birth of freedom; / and that government of the people, by the people, for the people, shall not perish from the earth.

Reading time: 45 seconds

17

Unfortunately, reading has fallen into disfavor among a significant portion of the population. Today, tens of millions of adults in the United States are *functionally illiterate*. Moreover, nearly 70 percent of high school students need some kind of remedial help because they cannot comprehend the words they read. Sadly, one million students come out of our public schools every year with poor reading skills. Because of this trend, the whole nation is being easily swayed by subtle forms of propaganda—through television and radio—because this segment of society cannot read or write. Television viewing obviously caters to the poor reader, who is bored and is easily amused. Unfortunately, **the desire to analyze**—an important skill for any good reader—has been nearly destroyed by television. However, this skill can be recaptured by a love for words and books. Seek to develop the habit of reading today.

CHAPTER TWO

IMPROVING
YOUR WRITING SKILLS

*Ideas put to paper and acted upon with the highest of energy
and uncompromising zeal can change the world. Even the worst
ideas have been used for this very purpose. If minds are going to be
transformed and civilizations changed, then Christians must learn
to write and write well. Writing is a sword, mightier than all the
weapons of war, because writing carries with it ideas that penetrate
deeper than any bullet. Writing about the right things in the right
way can serve as an antidote to the writings of skepticism and tyranny that have plundered the hearts and minds of generations of
desperate people around the world....*

Gary DeMar

The written word can and does change the way people think and
act. The most obvious example is how the Bible has impacted Western
civilization in the areas of literature, modern science, education, law,
medicine, and government. As Christ has transformed individual lives
by grace through faith, so those same individuals have influenced the
way we think and act today. As Abraham Lincoln has correctly stated in
regard to the Bible, "All the good from the Saviour of the world is communicated through this Book; but for the Book we could not know
right from wrong. All the things desirable to man are contained in it."

Writing is an art that can be mastered by anyone, even if a person
muses: "I can *never* learn to write!" However, you *can* learn to write
and do it well, so even the average person on the street can understand.
Expressing your ideas in a coherent and logical way is the most important goal. Style is a vital aspect, but *readability* is more important. So
put aside all negative thoughts about your writing ability and focus on
the positive aspects of learning new skills. And remember: *practice* is the
key. Writing skills cannot be cultivated in one brief sitting; therefore,
practice on a regular basis.

Starting a paper or essay for the budding writer is like going to the gym or health club for the first time. Your muscles are stiff and your breath is depleted after a three-minute workout; but in time, your stiffness and wheezing dissipates. So it is with your first attempts at writing; you will probably be rigid and awkward. Don't be discouraged! Use that frustration, and those negative thoughts, as a signal to change your approach. Look for new and better ways to sharpen your skills. The best place to start is with the skill of writing short, coherent sentences.

1. ACQUIRING SENTENCE CLARITY

Before becoming a good writer, you must be able to write a good sentence. Such a sentence expresses an idea by combining a *subject* and a *verb*. Thousands of students do not comprehend this simple fact, which results in countless mistakes in writing and speaking. It should also be noted, when you use compound and complex sentences, make sure that your *modifiers*—words, phrases, or clauses—express some relationship to the subject or verb.

One of the most important writing skills you can acquire is the ability to communicate an idea in a well-constructed sentence. We are often mesmerized by the ease of a writer or a speaker who knows how to express ideas and concepts in clear, meaningful sentences. It is rare to find a person who can rise at any given occasion and sway the opinion of a group one way or the other by a few well-designed, clear-cut sentences. Likewise, it is hard to find a student who can reason in clear, well-formed sentences regarding a part of an assignment, a book that has been read, or an event that has been attended. The whole structure of our language is built on the solid foundation of **sentence clarity**. So we must seek to cultivate this skill.

Acquiring the art of sentence clarity is no easy task. The greatest number of errors made by students—no matter what their age—can be traced back to a lack of sentence sense. The two most common errors are *run-on sentences* and *incomplete sentences*. The **run-on sentence** contains an excessive number of coordinating conjunctions (*and, but, or, nor, for, yet*) or misplaced commas. A run-on sentence may be defined as two or more sentences written incorrectly as one sentence. Some think that such sentences can be correctly written with only a comma between the sentences. This error is called a *comma splice*. Others think that punctuation is not necessary at all between sentences; however, this error produces the so-called *fused sentence*.

Run-on sentences may be corrected in the following ways:

1. If the sentences contain separate and distinct ideas, create two separate sentences, using a *period* and a *capital letter*.
2. If the ideas in the sentences are closely related and equally important, use a *comma* and a *coordinating conjunction* to properly form the sentence.
3. If the ideas in the sentences are closely related and equally important, you may also use a *semicolon*—dividing these ideas into two complete sentences.
4. Finally, if the ideas in the sentences are closely related but are *not* equally important, you may choose to *subordinate* the less important sentence; that is, to make the less important sentence into a dependent or subordinate clause.

The **incomplete sentence** is a group of words that does not contain a complete thought. This is sometimes called an *elliptical clause*, or an adverb clause, in which the subject or verb is supposedly understood. However, the subject or verb is often left *dangling*, which means that the writer has omitted what he actually intended to express. Such an incomplete sentence or elliptical clause may lead to ambiguity and misunderstanding. The best way for the budding "wordsmith" to write properly is by formulating each thought in a complete sentence—that is, with a subject and a verb. It should be noted, however, that essential parts of an elliptical clause may properly be omitted—only if *no* misunderstanding will occur. Therefore, incomplete sentences may be corrected in the following ways:

1. Always write each sentence out in a *complete thought*, using a subject and a verb. In this way you will not leave any room for misunderstanding.
2. For incomplete clauses beginning with *than* or *as*, use the pronouns that you would normally use if the clause was completed. For example:
   Mom can cook as well *as **they** [can]*.
   The drought affected the farmers more *than [it affected]* **us.**
3. Avoid *dangling elliptical clauses*. Correct this adverb clause by supplying the missing word(s). Sometimes this independent clause will have to be reworded completely.
4. Finally, if you choose to use an *elliptical clause*, make sure that the essential parts are properly omitted—leaving no ambiguity whatsoever.

Examine these well-constructed sentences: simple and complex.

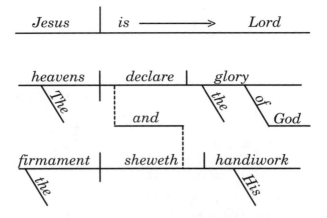

Figure 2.1 Sentence Outlining

The following ideas will help you to write clear, precise sentences:

1. **Write complete thoughts**—not just words—as you learn to compose each new sentence.
2. **Write one idea at a time** in each sentence when you correspond by letter or compose an essay.
3. **Write your thoughts in an orderly way**—in chronological order or how the subject develops logically—especially when you tell about an event, report on a plan, or describe an object.
4. **Write each sentence appropriately.** If it is a *declarative sentence* it tells something; if it is an *interrogative sentence* it asks something; if it is an *exclamatory sentence* it expresses strong emotion. Note, each kind of sentence ends with a particular punctuation mark.
5. **Write clauses or phrases correctly**—not in the form of independent sentences or *dangling elliptical clauses*, phrases, or sentences.
6. **Write each sentence with clarity.** Break up *run-on sentences* into one or more sentences, and rewrite *incomplete sentences*.
7. **Write sentences using proper connectives** (such as *that, when, as, which, who, where*) rather than short, choppy ones.
8. **Write compound and complex sentences** instead of only simple ones as you develop your sentence-writing skills.
9. **Write each sentence using variety**, especially when you begin a sentence. Help improve your style of writing and speaking by varying the order within your sentences, as well.

Examine the following revisions and check for sentence clarity.

Run-on sentence	There comes a time when each of must go our *add a colon* (:) *here* separate ways^ a child going away to college, a son or daughter getting married, changing jobs, or moving to another part of the country. Even people like the colonists came to the point of shedding their political
Choppy sentences	*add period, remove* 'and' & *cap.* 'The' ties with each of their homelands^ and ^the *Declaration of Independence* was their way of stating the necessity of beginning a new nation based on "the Laws of Nature and Nature's God." They gave specific reasons for why they were compelled to break
Run-on sentence	*add period here* & *remove* 'and' "political bands" that had bound them together ^ and *cap* 'The' ^the main reason for separation set forth was that all of them had been "created equal," and this equality had been bestowed upon them by their Creator, who has given them certain rights that cannot be taken
Incomplete sentence	*add verb*: 'are' away. Among them ^ the just claims to "life, liberty, and the pursuit of happiness." This is why the colonists wanted to separate and form a new government—separate from England—so they could secure
Misspelling	*change to* 'ie' these "inalêinable rights."

No one will ever learn to write or speak effectively if he fails to scrutinize, proofread, and rewrite his own work. Revising is an important step in learning to write better sentences.

2. Building a Paragraph

Just as you put words together to create a sentence, you join sentences together to *build a paragraph.* A paragraph is simply a group of sentences that develop one main idea or topic. The average person can write a single sentence, but only the individual who uses his mind can put several sentences together to make a paragraph—developing one topic in a logical, effective way. A paragraph contains *a topic sentence, supporting sentences* to the topic sentence, and sometimes a *summary sentence.* Good paragraphs are arranged and developed according to a definite course of action.

What would you think if you saw an automobile zigzagging down the road? Perhaps you would conclude that the car was either out of control or the driver was being reckless. Poor writing may be depicted in the same way—perhaps the writer does not have a *goal* or destination in mind when he starts out. Without such a goal, he will begin to zigzag all over the page, leaving the reader a bit "carsick." However, the goal of a good writer is called the *topic* or the main idea of the paragraph. The **topic sentence** is usually the first sentence of the paragraph, but for variety's sake it may be placed in the middle or at the end of the paragraph. Occasionally, the topic sentence may be implied; therefore, it is not written.

To develop a good paragraph, the writer must form well-written **supporting sentences** containing specific details that will support the main idea of the topic sentence. A well-built paragraph must have oneness, cohesion, and the proper stress. *Oneness* means that every sentence in the paragraph builds upon the one idea revealed in the topic sentence. Any sentence that does not support this main idea should be deleted. Likewise, the details you choose to support the topic must be in such good order and so clearly interrelated that the reader knows exactly what you mean. This is called *cohesion*—the quality of being logically integrated, consistent, as well as understandable. Furthermore, a paragraph gains the proper *stress* when the importance of each point in the paragraph is emphasized in some way. One way to stress a given point is by placing it at the beginning or end of the paragraph. Alternately, each point may be developed at a length proportionate to its importance.

The following are four ways a paragraph may be constructed to produce oneness, cohesion, and stress:

1. *Giving Examples*—Selected details are used to show the nature or character of the main idea expressed in the topic sentence. Each example should be like a "window" that sheds "light" on the main idea of the paragraph.

2. *Telling Incidents*—Events or anecdotes are employed to reveal certain aspects of the topic. These occurrences may be minor events or episodes that happen as a result of, or in connection with, something more important.

3. *Giving Reasons*—Explanations are used to justify the topic. The reasons are presented in such a way to help the reader to form particular judgments or draw certain conclusions.

4. *Comparing and Contrasting Subjects*—Similarities and differences between two or more subjects are developed by comparison and contrast. You should select significant points of comparison directly related to your purpose, and then develop them on an individual basis.

When developing a good paragraph, remember that you may arrange your details chronologically (according to time), descriptively (according to space), or imperatively (according to importance). In any event, the arrangement must have a definite order that either leads to a climax or produces the desired stress. Furthermore, to help your ideas flow smoothly from one sentence to the next, use such devices as *antecedent pronouns* (pronouns that refer to nouns in a preceding sentence), *repetition of key ideas* (words or phrases that are used repeatedly), and *transitional terms* (such as *accordingly, consequently, for example, however, namely, nevertheless, then, therefore,* and *thus*). These devices will help build congruity between your sentences. The arrangement of your details and the employment of these unifying devices will give your paragraph the proper stress, cohesion, and oneness.

Finally, to end a paragraph, a clincher or **summarizing sentence** is sometimes used. If the paragraph is long, then this sentence will tie all the supporting details together. Above all, it should restate the topic sentence used earlier, or like in the preceding paragraph, it is the topic sentence.

Here is an easy plan to follow in writing a paragraph:

1. *First*, your main idea or topic sentence must be given.
2. *Second*, the details need to develop your topic sentence with:
   - Examples,
   - Incidents,
   - Reasons, or
   - Comparisons and contrasts.
3. *Finally*, your conclusion or summary sentence should be stated.

Guidelines for writing a good paragraph:

1. *Write the topic sentence* making sure you treat only one aspect of your subject.

2. *List details*—as many as you possibly can on a separate page, without stopping to analyze each one. But make sure they support the topic.

3. *Eliminate any unrelated ideas* from the list that might be confusing to your reader.

4. *Select the most persuasive details,* while being mindful of your audience.

5. *Place details in a definite order,* either chronologically, spatially, or with respect to the significance of each detail.

6. *Write the first draft* of your paragraph, using every other line. Do this as rapidly as possible. Go back at a later time to find the right word or correct spelling. Do not stop to fix a garbled sentence or to look for more supportive material. *Push ahead to the end of the paragraph,* and overcome the tendency to perfect each sentence—no matter how clumsy or inadequate the wording may have become.

7. *Rewrite the paragraph.* Setting grammar aside for the moment, focus on the details and the order. Does the paragraph have oneness? Does it have cohesion? Does it have the proper stress? In addition, are the sentences clear, complete, and effective? *Remove, add, or rearrange as many items as needed*—even make an outline to help you clear up any ambiguity that has crept in.

8. *Edit the paragraph.* Now you should go back and examine everything in the minutest detail. *Check each paragraph for oneness, cohesion, and proper stress.* Next check each sentence to see if it is correct, clear, and effective. Finally, grammar, mechanics, phrases, individual words, and spelling must all be examined and corrected if necessary.

9. *Write the final copy.* Be sure that the paragraph is neat and properly indented. Also be sure that the margins are set according to specifications.

Here are two selections that illustrate how a well-written paragraph should be composed:

From: *George Washington the Christian*
by William J. Johnson

Topic sentence

Support sentences

Summary sentence

During his residence in Philadelphia, as President of the United States, it was the habit of Washington, winter and summer, to retire to his study at a certain hour every night. He usually did so at nine o'clock— always having a lighted candle in hand, and closing the door carefully after him. A youthful member of the household whose room was near the study, being just across the passage, observing this constant practice of the President, had his thoughts excited in reference to the cause of so uniform a custom. Thus, on one occasion, in the indulgence of a juvenile curiosity, he looked into the room, some time after the President had gone in; and to his surprise, saw him upon his knees at a small table, with a candle and open Bible thereon.

From: *Iron Scouts of the Confederacy*
by Lee McGriffin

Topic sentence

Vivid details

Yet, as the days passed, he realized that the Iron Scouts were not really a part of the boisterous camp life. They came and went like shadows. Some of the lean-faced men of the plains did not come back. Some of the far-seeing mountain men returned from Yankee prisons, their faces pale, their tough bodies thinned. Some of the hunters from the far away hills were buried where they fell behind Yankee lines.
(*Note: there is no summary sentence.*)

3. Crafting an Outline

Every year Detroit puts out the latest model cars—which does not happen overnight. Each new car is built from a carefully devised scheme. In the same way, a builder must have a blueprint to construct a house. A craftsman also needs a sketch or scale drawing when creating a masterpiece. An **outline** is just such a plan for the writer or speaker who wants to craft an essay or speech. No one can hold an audience unless a person knows what he is talking about. Therefore, be sure that you make an *outline* whenever you sit down to write a theme or formulate a speech.

Use the following rules when making an outline:

1. *Select a subject.* Choose one that is not too broad to be adequately covered in the allotted space or time. If necessary, narrow the subject to a manageable size. Write out a statement of purpose, explaining how you are going to tackle the subject.
2. *Make a list of ideas* that support the main topic. Compare each idea with the statement of purpose, and cross off any unrelated or dubious thoughts.
3. *Choose the main headings* from your list or your creative thought processes. In either case, refer to your statement of purpose as your guide. Group the remaining ideas under the main headings. *Determine what the subheadings* and supporting details are going to be, then arrange them in some kind of order.
4. **Roman numerals** (I, II, III, etc.) are used to highlight main ideas, where each is written in a similar way. The best approach is to compose a complete sentence, or a concise phrase. Use capital letters at the beginning of each sentence or phrase.
5. **Capital letters** (A, B, C, etc.) indicate each of the subtopics, which are indented under the Roman numerals. There must be at least two subheadings under each main idea.
6. **Arabic numerals** (1, 2, 3, etc.) mark off the details under each subtopic, which are indented under the capital letters. There should be at least two supporting details for every subheading.
7. *Arrange the main ideas in a logical order* (chronologically, spatially, or in the order of their importance). Your outline needs to reflect a unified and coherent plan of execution.

Your outline serves as a *road map* for getting you to your desired destination. Hopefully, you will lead your audience to the same conclusion. An outline is a logical exercise toward that end—cutting through your own confusion about the topic. Therefore, your "road map" will vary depending on your subject matter. Your itinerary may follow a historical progression, a comparative analysis, or a thematic development. But in any case, your outline will always cover three main sections: the *introduction*, the *body*, and the *conclusion*. Save the introduction and conclusion for last. Concentrate on the body of the paper, and use your outline as a tool to get you where you want to go.

Review the following outline that was derived from an article written by Gary DeMar. This is a suggested plan that outlines the opening third of the chapter entitled "God Is Sovereign, Not Man," taken from DeMar's work called *Ruler of the Nations* (Dominion Press, 1987). Note the placement of the Roman numerals, capital letters, and Arabic numerals according to their impact and overall support of the main topic.

Main Topic: "God Is Sovereign, Not Man"*

I. Introduction
  A. Negative Example:
    Herod—falsely worshipped as a god
    1. The people trusted Herod like a god.
    2. Americans trust in the god of money.
  B. Positive Example:
    First Commandment—true worship of God
    1. The God of the Bible is sovereign.
    2. Biblical covenant structure supports this.
  C. Older Definition of "Government":
    Biblical government is Christ's rule, alone.
    1. Webster's definition of true government
    2. The singular government of Jesus Christ
II. The One Government of God
  A. God as the Model for All Types of Governing:
    1. Government of the individual
    2. Government of the family
    3. Government of the church
    4. Government of the nation
  B. The One and the Many:
    Etc.

4. Developing a Theme

Printing has changed for the better over the years. When Johann Gutenberg first invented the printing press more than 550 years ago, the printer's page was entirely covered with type. Indentations were nonexistent, so any breaks in thought were difficult to determine. Therefore, reading with understanding was arduous. But today every story, news article, or piece of nonfiction is divided into carefully marked paragraphs. The reader can easily trace the author's flow of thought, moving from one paragraph to another.

A story or news article may be categorized as a **theme**, defined as a full-length composition. A *theme* consists of several paragraphs—each one linked to the following paragraph, much like the links of a chain. As a chain has a beginning and an ending coupling, so a theme has an

---

* This article can be found in Appendix 2 of *The Land of Fair Play*, Third Edition (Arlington Heights, IL: Christian Liberty Press, 2008).

introductory and a concluding paragraph. The key to writing a good theme is found in learning a few basic skills in how to link each "coupling" into a full-length "chain."

Many of the same principles that apply to writing a good paragraph also pertain to developing a full-length composition. The *first* step is to select a **subject** that is interesting to you and, at the same time, appealing to the general reader. *Second*, the subject should be limited in scope: it is better to write "more about less" than to write "less about more." After choosing your subject, the most important task is stating your **purpose**. This sentence should capture your main thought and give your idea direction. Taking time to fix your purpose in exact terms will go a long way in helping you save time and write a better paper.

Third, organize your **ideas**. With your purpose statement in hand, write down as many related ideas as you can. Initially, make a list of these items and do not worry about the order. You may have to do some research to supplement your immediate knowledge on the subject. The more supporting material you find, the better. Cross off all unrelated or dubious ideas. Compare each idea in the list with your statement of purpose. Do not be afraid to cut any superfluous ideas, even if you have to do more research to fill out your list. When this process is complete, fit these points into an **outline** format. Determine the main headings—using Roman numerals—and group the remaining ideas under each of these headings. Decide which points will become subheadings—using capital letters indented under the main headings. Then arrange the main points and subpoints either chronologically, spatially, or in the order of their importance.

The *fourth* step is to write the **first draft**, which includes the introduction, the body, and the conclusion. All three of these parts are vital in the writing of an effective composition, so do not neglect them. The *introduction* varies in size depending on the length of your assignment. A long composition may have two paragraphs in the introduction, while an essay would need only one paragraph. The whole idea, though, is to capture your reader's attention, leading him into your subject. A startling fact, a provocative anecdote, a weighty quotation, a cogent opinion, or a riveting prediction are all possible ways of introducing your subject and captivating your reader.

The *body* of the theme is the heart of your paper, being developed from your outline. To maintain the proper emphasis, give the most important points more space. On your outline, mark off the points that you plan to include in each paragraph, which will help to keep your first draft flowing. Above all, get your ideas on paper first; then develop each paragraph later. Similarly, the transitions are vital because they tie the various paragraphs together in a unified, coherent way.

The following chart lists some common words or phrases that can be used as transitions:

Category	Transitional Expressions
Time	first, second, third, finally, in the first place, next, then, meanwhile, in the meantime
Space	here, nearby, above, below, beside, beyond
Addition	and, moreover, in addition, similarly, again, besides
Contrast	but, yet, nor, on the other hand, nevertheless, on the contrary, however
Alternative	otherwise, whereas, else
Repetition	in fact, in short, that is, in other words
Result	consequently, therefore, thus, hence, accordingly, as a result

Figure 2.2 Transitions

The *conclusion* rounds out your composition, leaving your reader with the assurance that you have met your goal. The topic sentence of this paragraph should reflect your original purpose statement, but in a modified way. This can be expanded with a probable result, an item of significance, an apt quotation, a prophetic warning, an engaging anecdote, or a powerful summary. This is the time to bring your point home.

Fifth, **rewrite** your composition and determine whether the work is complete or not. Ask yourself these five questions: (1) Is everything you need included? (2) Are all the parts in the proper order? (3) Is the paper unified, with all extraneous details removed? (4) Does the thought flow smoothly from one paragraph to the next? (5) Has each part been developed at an appropriate length in proportion to its importance? Continue to rewrite each subsequent draft until you have satisfied the above five questions. When the final draft is complete, the writer assumes the role of an editor.

Step *six* is where you should goes back and **edit** everything in the minutest detail. Check each *paragraph* for oneness, cohesion, and stress. Then tackle each *sentence* for correctness, grammar, and mechanics. The *phrases* also need to be examined for the proper figure of speech and expression of idiom. Eliminate inappropriate jargon, trite phrases, and wordiness. This whole discussion leads us next to *words*. Check to see that your verbs are bright and alive, and that your nouns are specific and direct. Above all, see that they are used in an appropriate way—particularly in regard to your audience. Make sure all words are spelled correctly. After all changes have been made, you will be ready to begin the final copy.

The *seventh* step involves the **final draft**. At this time, you should choose an appropriate title for your paper. Keep in mind your subject and purpose, as well as your audience. You want to seize your reader's interest in a concise, yet descriptive way. After you have chosen a suitable title, neatly write the final copy of your composition. Proofread it for mechanical accuracy (title page, spacing, margins, indentations, and page numbering), and examine the overall appearance of your paper for legibility. Then read your completed composition, and make any adjustments that are necessary. Plan, write, rewrite, edit, proofread, and finalize—these are the tasks of a good writer.

Here are several suggestions for your next writing assignment:

Topics for Compositions

1.	Airplanes or jets	14.	News commentators
2.	Boats or ships	15.	Omniscience of God
3.	Cars or vans	16.	Propaganda
4.	Drug abuse	17.	Qumran Scrolls
5.	Electrical power	18.	Resurrection of Jesus
6.	Futuristic design	19.	Swimming strokes
7.	Guns or weapons	20.	Transfusion of blood
8.	Hymns or songs	21.	Undercover agents
9.	Influenza or viruses	22.	Violation of the law
10.	Jesus as God & man	23.	War & revolution
11.	Kangaroos & koalas	24.	X-rays or radiation
12.	Literature & art	25.	Yellowstone Park
13.	Musical instruments	26.	Zwingli–reformer

Figure 2.3

5. Proofreading Your Work

Everyone is occasionally amused by some printing error or mis-spelled word in a headline of a newspaper or on a billboard. Perhaps you have seen a sign that reads: "**PLAN AHEAD**"—but the last few letters are in a squeezed, dangling sort of pattern due to poor planning! Obviously, no one is perfect—but the prudent person seeks to correct his mistakes before submitting the finished product.

Few people can write a note, essay, or narrative without making some kind of spelling error or thoughtless oversight. To eliminate mis-takes in spelling, punctuation, or capitalization, you need to proofread everything you write. Continuous checking and correcting of errors—both of omission or commission—will make you a better writer.

When you are proofreading, heed the following guidelines:

1. **Examine each sentence.** Be sure that run-on sentences have been eliminated and all sentences are complete.
2. **Examine all verbs.** Make sure that the subject and the verb agree with each other, and that the correct form of the verb is always employed.
3. **Examine punctuation marks.** Check all the punctuation that was used; make any adjustments that are needed to correct the marks for the proper stress. Remember, independent clauses are separated by a comma and a coordinating conjunction or by a semicolon.
4. **Examine capitalization.** Adjust run-on sentences by breaking them apart and capitalizing the start of each new sentence. Also, look for words that are improperly capitalized; change them to the lower case.
5. **Examine the spelling of words.** You should make *good spelling* a goal. Word-processing and computer programs have built-in "spell check" capabilities. However, you should choose a par-ticular hardbound dictionary (e.g., *Merriam-Webster's Collegiate Dictionary*) or online dictionary (e.g., <www.merriam-webster. com>) as your standard. Also remember that a "spell check" pro-gram will not catch a misspelled word if the misspelling has cre-ated another word.
6. **Examine each paragraph.** Each paragraph should have one main topic. If you have more than one topic in any given paragraph, separate the paragraph into two units.
7. **Revise your work.** Correct any errors you find in your compo-sition. Rewrite your first draft, occasionally substituting one word for another—especially those that are used repeatedly. Your *thesaurus* is a good source to help infuse some variety into your style of writing.

One of the best ways to proofread your work is to simply *read aloud* the final product and *listen* to the words and the flow of thought. Recording your essay or paper may also help you analyze it more objectively. Listening to what you have composed can aid you in examining your style, clarity, accuracy, and development of thought. You could even have a friend or relative critique your final draft—an outside perspective is always a good way to catch any oversights of grammar, spelling, or punctuation.

If time permits, set your paper aside for a couple of days, and then come back to it for your final analysis. After you have made all the necessary adjustments, reread the final draft, making sure you included all the revisions. Check for any new errors that may have crept in.

The following example is an excerpt from a story called "Respect for the Sabbath Rewarded."*

(Verb correction)	*walked* One Sunday evening, a stranger ~~walk~~ up to the market house from one of the cabs and asked where he could find a barber. He was directed by an elderly woman
(Better word)	*to* ~~for~~ the little cellar shop. Coming in hastily, he requested to be shaved quickly, as he did not like to violate the Sabbath. This comment touched the barber on a tender chord. He burst into tears and
(Omission)	*lend* asked the stranger to ^ him a dime to buy a candle, as it was not light enough to shave him with safety. He did so, while considering in his mind
(Noun clarification)	*poor barber* the extreme poverty to which the ~~man~~ was reduced. He could not even afford to properly light his shop.

---

* "Respect for the Sabbath Rewarded" is found in *McGuffey's Fifth Eclectic Reader* by William Holmes McGuffey (Cincinnati and New York: Van Antwerp, Bragg & Co., revised edition, 1879, pp 69, 70). Note: the "errors" that were *added* are not in the original text, but the "corrections" are part of the original text.

CHAPTER THREE

IMPROVING YOUR COMPOSITION SKILLS

Building on our basic writing skills, we now want to turn our attention to developing our composition skills. The word *composition* comes from the adjective "composite," which simply means "to put together." So, the act of composing is the combining of specific parts into a whole unit. The art of writing, therefore, is the putting together of words and thoughts to create a letter, speech, story, term paper, or manuscript. At some point in our lives, almost all of us will have to write a letter, give a speech, or put our thoughts down on paper. Therefore, we must build on sentence sense, paragraph construction, and theme development to compose our various forms of discourse.

1. COMPOSING A LETTER

When was the last time you sat down and *composed a letter*? Perhaps you do not have a pressing need now, but in the future you will no doubt have to correspond with a relative, contact a prospective employer, or communicate with your representative or senator in Congress. Some people enjoy writing personal letters, and do so on a regular basis. If you plan to go into business for yourself or decide to work for someone else, knowing how to handle correspondence in a professional way is an important skill to acquire.

Letters are more expressive perhaps than the most flattering photograph because they reveal more about you than you realize. They can either sell your personality or dash your ego to the ground. Therefore, studying creative letter writing will go a long way in helping you to articulate the image you want to project. Even the shortest note can make a world of difference, if it is composed properly. Study the following letters—the first is the friendly letter:

1445 Prospect Avenue
Newark, NJ 07107
March 22, 20--

Dear Suzanne,

Imagine my surprise when I received Mary's letter telling me about your summer plans! Then, two days later, your letter arrived and gave me further details.

You and Mary evidently are going to keep busy, but that's the way a vacation ought to be. While you are in Chicago, however, I hope that you find time to look up Jill Hughes, who is one of my dearest friends. I'm sure she will give you and Mary a big welcome.

On the index card enclosed, I am providing Jill's address and telephone number, as well as a few facts about her family. I hope that you will have time to make good use of the information; if not, I will understand.

In your letter, you inquired about Mark Young. He is no longer living in Chicago. He and his family moved to St. Louis last September, so you won't have an opportunity to see him during your trip.

Please be sure to send me a card from Chicago to let me know how you like my home city.

Have a wonderful trip.

Cordially,

Cheri Jordan

Enclosure

999 Central Park Drive
Worchester, MA 01601
March 22, 20--

Mr. John McDonnelly
Personnel Manager
Publishers International, Inc.
5000 Commonwealth Avenue
Boston, MA 02109-5000

Dear Mr. McDonnelly:

In Monday's *Daily Tribune*, I read your advertisement for the position of secretary. May I please be considered an applicant for this position?

In June, I will graduate from high school with a 3.5 grade point average. As you will see on the enclosed personal data sheet, I have earned 8 elective credits in business and art courses. I feel my extensive technical skills in word processing and business communications, and my knowledge of color and art layout will be an excellent background for working as a secretary for Publishers International.

For the past two summers, I have worked doing data entry for several companies through the Youth Development Program sponsored by the Department of Employment. Each summer, I worked for three weeks at four different companies, where I had the opportunity to use my skills and to learn actual office procedures. During this school year, I have worked part-time at my father's company as a switchboard operator answering calls and taking messages.

I would appreciate having a personal interview at a time that is mutually convenient. I can be reached at 345-9876.

Sincerely,

(Miss) Teri R. Greene

999 Central Park Drive
Worchester, MA 01601

Mr. John McDonnelly
Personnel Manager
Publishers International, Inc.
5000 Commonwealth Avenue
Boston, MA 02109-5000

2. Presenting a Short Speech

Have you ever been asked to give a brief discourse or talk? Or have you been called upon to teach a Sunday School class or to say a few words at a special occasion? The ability to write and deliver a *short speech* is one of the most valuable skills you can acquire. As you continue through life, you will be granted various opportunities to speak before an audience.
The ability to give such a talk will go a long way in assisting you to make new friends, to sell a certain product, to promote a critical idea, or to advance in business, politics, or society in general.

First, you must be able to plan and draft a speech, prior to its delivery. You must also be a student of your audience—knowing their interests, biases, and concerns. It could be that your listeners are junior high students; then you would talk on a subject with which they will identify. If your group is made up of sixth-grade boys who are assembled for a Bible class, then you should address the Scriptures in a way that will captivate their way of thinking. Maybe you have been asked to present a eulogy for a close friend or relative, so you could choose your words in a way that would convey the right message to everyone present. Perhaps these very words will make the greatest impact on their lives for eternity—especially if they are seeking answers to the most important questions in life.

Here are some helpful guidelines:

1. **Choose a subject** that is of interest to both you and your audience. Avoid negative attitudes. Do not wait till the last minute to choose a topic either.
2. **Select a specific purpose** for which the subject is going to be addressed. Ask yourself: "What do I expect my audience to do in regard to this subject?" Make sure your listeners are actively involved with this specific purpose.
3. **Gather detailed ideas** and visual aids for your subject. Recalling personal experiences, listening to others, observing the world around us, and reading good books are superb ways to begin. Definitions, examples, quotations, and even statistics will also enhance your presentation. Do not be afraid to utilize charts, maps, diagrams, pictures, slides, or video to your advantage.
4. **Write a good beginning sentence.** Capture the attention of your audience, and entice them to hear more. The words that come out of your mouth first make all the difference in the world.

5. **Make a goal of writing events in their proper order.** If you are describing the location of certain details, they should be presented from near to far, top to bottom, right to left, or from the center to the periphery. If you are developing the subject by reasons or examples, they should be dealt with in the order of their importance. If time is a factor, use chronological order.

6. **Organize your thoughts into an outline:** introduction, body, and conclusion. *First* you get your listeners' attention, introduce the subject, and create interest; *secondly,* the body should be arranged in some logical sequence, and any visual aids should be wisely placed; and *finally,* you conclude with a summary that impacts your audience and ties up loose ends.

7. **List the details under each main point** for a complete description. Check for variety, oneness, cohesion, and the proper stress. All of your details should build up toward a climax, which should receive the most emphasis in content and delivery.

8. **Keep your surprise near the end.** If at all possible, the bulk of your speech should work cogently toward the "bombshell" you plan to drop at the end.

9. **Put your finalized speech on note cards** in numerical sequence, including your opening and closing statements. Your outline or key ideas of what you want to say should also be organized on note cards. Number them to maintain the right order.

10. **Choose an appropriate title for your speech.** It may be one word or a phrase; nevertheless, it must capture the subject and purpose in a nutshell.

Now you are ready to *practice the delivery* of your speech. Try to relax and concentrate on speaking clearly, accurately, and with the proper emphasis. Make sure that what you say is understandable and that you have enough illustrative material. Simple, straightforward sentences, repetition of key ideas, and clear transitional expressions also go a long way toward enriching your presentation. *Speak loudly and clearly.* Slow down if you are speaking too fast; you want your audience to keep pace. But do not put them to sleep, either; use variety in the tone of your voice, especially if you want to stress a particular point.

Eye contact, gestures, and *facial expressions* can all be effectively used in reaching your audience. Practice using your visual aids so that you will be able to integrate them with ease into your speech. During your presentation, try to notice the reactions of those listening; this important feedback will help you make the necessary adjustments as you go along. Last but not least, use those anxious thoughts and the excitement of the moment to your advantage to energize your talk.

Sir Winston Churchill gave the following address before the House of Commons on June 4, 1940, almost one year after World War II had begun (September 1,1939). This is a powerful example of what a short speech should be—exhibiting the ten guidelines mentioned on the previous page. Note the wise use of repetition and the call to the "New World" to help the old:

"The Resolution"
by Sir Winston Churchill

We shall not flag or fail. We shall go on to the end, we shall fight in France, we shall fight on the seas and oceans, we shall fight with growing confidence and growing strength in the air, we shall defend our island, whatever the cost may be, we shall fight on the beaches, we shall fight on the landing grounds, we shall fight in the fields and in the streets, we shall fight in the hills; we shall never surrender, and even if, which I do not for a moment believe, this Island or a large part of it were subjugated and starving, then our Empire beyond the seas, armed and guarded by the British Fleet, would carry on the struggle, until, in God's good time, the New World, with all its power and might, steps forth to the rescue and the liberation of the old.

3. Creating a Short Story

Creative writing is a craft in which an author invents characters, situations, images, and emotions; subsequently, they are put into stories, novels, plays, and poems. However, you might ask, what arouses one's imagination to create such characters or images? Perhaps a picture in a magazine sparks your inner thoughts, which in turn, helps your creativity to shift into gear. Maybe the aroma of freshly baked bread gets your creative juices flowing, and you recall a past event that inspires your pen to abound with vibrant ideas. In any case, you are the one that animates your imagination—visualizing an intriguing hideaway or conjuring up some mystifying dilemma.

So it is with writing a *short story*. Your story might grow out of a small event in your own life that tugs at your imaginative resources. From this experience, you start to invent a series of happenings that are all connected together in some way. No matter how you begin, you will be constructing your narrative with the following elements, which are found in all good stories: a *plot*, one or more *characters*, a *setting*, a *narrator*, and a *theme*.

Basic Elements of a Short Story

1. The **plot** is a sequence of events that build up to a *crisis* or point of climax. Your plot should develop some kind of *tension* or dilemma. This discord may occur between two individuals, between one person and some outside force, or within the soul of a person.
2. The **character** or characters should have *personalities* with which your reader can identify—projecting credibility. Each one should also have a clear *motive* for his of her actions.
3. The **setting** is a key factor that gives your short story a *time frame* and *location* for the characters to develop. Make sure that the plot, the one or more characters, and the setting all fit together.
4. The **narrator** is the one through whom you tell the story. A *first person* narrator is a character within the story; however, a *third-person* narrator relates the thoughts of one or more characters from within or without the story.
5. Finally, the **theme** is the one controlling *thought* or *effect* of life that is suggested by a specific circumstance, person, and place from your story.

To begin writing your story, you need to *generate story ideas* by conjuring up intriguing people, places, and points of tension. Consult various sources for pictures and photographs that will become catalysts for the short story you are creating. Also, search your own thoughts for memories that you can develop into mini-stories. Then chart your results under three main headings: circumstances/tension, character(s), and setting. Each mini-story should contain these three elements.

After you have generated these story ideas, *examine* them one at a time. Create in your mind's eye the appearance and actions of each character within a particular setting. Examine these ideas for your story by following these steps below:

Developing the Basic Elements of a Short Story

- Decide why you want to examine each idea.
- Determine the *tension* that will exist between the characters and what the point of *crisis* will be.
- Choose your main *characters* and their ages.
- Create their overall appearances. Be specific about height, weight, coloring, features, and clothing.
- Bring their *personalities* to life through their speech and actions.
- Invent a *setting*, including a scene, time period, and climate.
- Select what kind of *narrator* would work well with this story.
- Develop a *theme* that will fit your storyline.

Next, generate an *outline* for your story by organizing your thoughts. Logically develop the main events in the plot, which will help you to clarify the sequence of these events and reveal your main characters. Use the following standard outline to plan your story:

I. Introduction
    A. **Present the main characters.**
    B. **Explain the setting.**
    C. **Set up the underlying circumstances.**

II. Body
    A. **Introduce the tension or dilemma.**
    B. **Animate the reaction of each character with respect to this tension.**
    C. **Build up to the crisis or point of climax.**

III. Conclusion
    A. **Initiate the crisis.**
    B. **Wind down the action.**
    C. **Reveal the end result.**

First, upon completing the above steps, you will be ready to write the **initial draft** of your story. Your narrator should introduce the characters by placing them in their proper setting so that your reader can immediately identify with them. If the narrator is one of the characters in your story, make his words convey his or her personality as well. First-person pronouns (*I, me*) should be used throughout for a first-person narrator; likewise, third-person pronouns (*he, she, it, they*) are employed for third-person or omniscient narration.

Second, let the words and actions of your characters speak for themselves—not you. For example, do not say, "Ben was angry," but let Ben show his anger by exploding or acting it out. Include **dialogue**, or conversation between the characters, whenever possible. This technique will make your story more vivid because it acquaints the reader with the actual words of the character. Also, remember to follow these guidelines when inventing dialogue between the characters:

1. Use **quotation marks** for all words spoken by the characters. Direct quotations may come at either the beginning or end of a sentence.
2. Direct quotations all begin with a capital letter. However, the second part of mid-sentence interruptions begin with a lower case letter.
3. Each time you change the person who is speaking, begin a new paragraph, and also begin a new paragraph when the narrative comes into play.
4. Use **commas** to set off direct quotations.

Third, create **excitement** in your story by generating tension and building a high level of anticipation. And by all means, make it a goal for your characters to behave in a way that is consistent with their personalities. As your story comes to a close, initiate the crisis—the high point of your story. Then wind down the tension by resolving the dilemma. An excellent way to end your story is to reveal what each character has come to realize about himself, in particular, or about life in general.

Last comes the **title, revisions, editing**, and ultimately the publishing of the story. The *title* needs to grab your reader's attention, so write one that is interesting, yet concise. Also make sure it refers back to some important event, character, place, or theme in your story. Once you have selected a title and finished your first draft, take time to improve your story until it satisfies your sense of rightness or propriety. Subsequently, read your story aloud or have a friend criticize your finished product. Then use the following checklist to help you *revise, edit, proofread*, and *publish* your writing:

1. Examine the *details* used to describe the setting. Are they adequate? If not, revise or add new ones.
2. Examine the *physical features* and *mannerisms*, underlying *motives*, and *personality traits* for each of the characters. Are they adequate? If not, make any necessary changes.
3. Examine the perspective of the *narrator* used in the story and make sure he stays within that perspective throughout.
4. Examine the *tension* that is introduced, built up, brought to a climax, and then resolved in the context of the story.
5. Examine *oneness* and *cohesion* of each event, making sure that they are tied together with what happened before and after.
6. Examine the *dialogue* you created, and try to make it sound more true to life. Use the correct format for each quotation.
7. Examine the *crisis* or point of climax of the story, determining how the *tension* or dilemma is to be resolved.
8. Examine the *language* you used. Are your nouns specific and direct, and are your verbs bright and alive?
9. Examine each sentence for completeness. Make sure you have avoided any errors in verbs, pronouns, and modifiers.
10. Examine your spelling, capitalization, and punctuation in each sentence; check spacing, indentation, and quotations.
11. Examine what might be a good place for presenting your completed story. Perhaps you could read it to your family, friends, or instructors, or possibly enter it in a contest.

The following story, "A Lesson About Friendship" is a good example of how to incorporate all the elements of a short story. After you have read through this exciting adventure, try your hand at writing one of your own.

"A Lesson About Friendship"*

Two friends were traveling together one day upon the same road, when they met a bear. One of the men, who was the younger and more active of the two, sprang up a tree and hid himself amongst its boughs. The other, seeing that he could do nothing to protect himself against the bear, was so overcome with fear that he sank to the ground. He remembered that his grandfather had once told him that bears would never touch a dead body. They prefer first to kill whatever animals they wish to eat.

With but a moment to think of how he could save his life, he threw himself upon the ground, and lay as though he were dead. Soon the bear came smelling and snuffing at the man's nose, ears, and heart, but the poor fellow held his breath and kept as still as death.

Finally, the bear made up his mind that the man was dead; and as bears do not care for anything they themselves have not killed, the big black fellow walked away.

As soon as the bear was out of sight, the man in the tree came down, saying to his friend, who had had such a narrow escape, "What did the bear say to you? I noticed he put his mouth very close to your ear."

"Why," replied the other, "it was no very great secret; for he said for me to be very careful hereafter how I kept company with those who would desert me in time of trouble."

---

* This short story is adapted from Æsop's fable called "The Bear and the Two Travelers."

4. Preparing a Book Report

Many people enjoy reading a good book—some read to unwind after a long, hard day; others read for the sake of gaining information and improving their minds; and many read to pursue a hobby or craft. Furthermore, some students read the greatest authors of the English-speaking world because their thoughts or stories have become a vital part of our everyday usage. Other students read books to gain knowledge in a particular area of study, especially if it relates to their immediate course work or future career goals. Thus, reading may be informative and enjoyable at the same time.

But you can go a step further and put your thoughts, attitudes, and feelings down on paper, in regard to a particular book you have just read. This is accomplished by writing a well-prepared *book report*. This exercise gives you the opportunity to tell whether you liked or disliked a book. More importantly, you can explain why you were enamored with a certain work, or repulsed by it—as the case may be. Initially, you need to acquaint yourself with the work. You obviously cannot evaluate a book that you have merely glanced over in a hasty manner. *Read the book carefully*; and then try to grasp the author's overall purpose and plot. Finally, write a review that includes an introduction, summary (or body), conclusion, and proof of thesis or evaluation.

First, your **introduction** should include *general information* and your *thesis statement*. In this initial paragraph, you should state the author's name and the title of the book; and you should determine whether it is fiction, biography, or informational. Get your readers hooked on what you are going to say—perhaps an engaging statement or quotation would do the trick. After these generalizations have been divulged, write your thesis statement, which declares your attitude toward the book and gives the main ideas you are going to amplify in the book report. This statement reveals your evaluation of the book.

Second, you will give a brief summary of the work, called the **body** of your report. Initially, state the setting, list the main characters, and write a descriptive paragraph about the most interesting character in the book. Do not lose your reader by retelling every incident in the story—but highlight the main events in your second paragraph. If you have read a biography, then relate the main events in the person's life that are important, and explain why they are significant. If you read a nonfiction book, explain why the subject matter is vital and summarize the various parts of the work. If you read a fiction title, briefly describe the plot or sequence of events—depicting the conflict between the characters or a character and his environment—that lead up to the climax.

Third, the **conclusion** follows by giving a general restatement of the thesis. In regard to a biography, you would state the significance of the person's life that has been retold. In regard to a nonfiction book, the major points of the text should be summarized, supporting the author's main purpose. And in regard to a fiction title, you need to explain the the events that resolve the conflict—after the climax has been revealed. Be sure to include the overall theme of the story. In your own words give what you believe the author is trying to express through the events in the book—the moral of the story.

Fourth, the next several paragraphs should disclose your evaluation in detail. This **proof of thesis** or evaluation should be fair and accurate, following the information you gathered from your appraisal of the purpose, organization, style, vividness, and truthfulness of the book. Prove your thesis by using specific incidents from the work itself. Initially, you must discern the author's *purpose*, or intentions. The author wants to persuade his audience to accept his particular point of view, so he must keep a clear vision of that purpose or opinion. If the author's purpose is sharply disclosed, then you will be able to easily determine his intentions.

Next ask yourself if he fulfilled that purpose through proper *organization*. The author should have a clear, well-developed plot. Make sure that he has only included what was necessary—not cluttering the book with needless events or unrelated details. If he has included any unnecessary information, make note of it in your critique.

Your evaluation must go deeper than the writer's general purpose and outline. Take a closer look at the *style*, or overall beauty, of the work. Examine the language used to see if it has depth, or perhaps the author has been superficial, demonstrated in his use of trite expressions or overdone clichés. Good descriptions, comparisons, and symbolism are all earmarks of good style. Closely tied to the style of an author is the *vividness* of his language. Judge whether or not the words used are full of life, color, and import. Do the characters have personalities that are bright and alive?

Also determine if the author has made these characters seem real to you the reader. And finally, has the author used *truthfulness*, or accuracy, in portraying the events or presenting the characters. If he has been consistent and truthful, specifically express these thoughts in your critique. However, if the writer has been less than truthful, expose the statements or expressions that support your claims.

Use the outline on the next two pages to write your book report. It should always be one and a half to two handwritten pages, unless you are directed differently. (Note: seventh grade students and above may choose to type their reports, if they are not instructed otherwise.)

I. The Introduction
   A. Begin with a sentence that includes the title of the book, the author's name, and the main idea the author is setting forth.
   B. Get your readers hooked on what you are going to say—perhaps you could write a striking statement or quotation.
   C. If the book has a noteworthy setting, you may want to include it. State the time and place of when and where the action took place.
   D. The thesis statement should be introduced here, declaring your attitude toward the book and the main ideas you will cover.
II. The Body
   A. If you have read a biography, relate the main events and explain their importance.
   B. If a nonfiction book is your choice, tell why the book's subject is important and develop a sketch of its various parts.
   C. If you are critiquing a fiction book, write a survey of the plot, including the conflict between two major or minor characters, or the main characters with other people or their environment. Recount the key events that develop the conflict—leading up to the climax.
   D. State the setting, list the main characters, and write a descriptive paragraph about the most interesting character in the book. Then summarize the plot.
III. The Conclusion
   A. In regard to a biography, your concluding sentences should cite the significance of the person's life as depicted in the book.
   B. In regard to a nonfiction book, your final sentences should summarize the major points in the text.
   C. In regard to a fictitious work, your conclusion should include the resolution of the tension that built up to the point of crisis.
   D. Above all, the conclusion should provide a concise summary of the author's theme. At this point, state what moral you think the author is trying to express through the events in the book.

IV. Proof of Thesis or Evaluation
   A. Reveal your personal reaction to the book, explaining what you liked or disliked. Describe your feelings with regard to the outcome—explain if it was satisfactory or not. If there was a specific need the author was trying to fulfill, explain whether or not it was met. Did the book change your way of thinking or your outlook on life? Give specific examples that support your point of view.
   B. Evaluate the purpose, organization, style, vividness, and truthfulness of the author. Your appraisal should be substantiated by specific incidents from the book itself.
   C. This evaluation should be written in a paragraph that is well-developed and should contain the bulk of your material.

Carefully examine the following example of a good, high school level book report. Review any other instructions that may be given in your course requirements before starting.

Not My Will*
by Francena H. Arnold

Introduction   <u>Not My Will</u> by Francena H. Arnold recounts the struggles and mishaps of young, determined Eleanor Stewart as she searches for true peace and happiness. Though saved at an early age, Eleanor is brought up in a non-Christian atmosphere and seems to have forgotten God. She is determined to succeed on her own and refuses to yield completely to the Lord. Throughout the book, she is experiencing a constant struggle within her own soul.

Body   Eleanor attends a prominent university in a large city. Her whole life seems to center on her school and laboratory work. So absorbed is she in this work that she does not even take time to participate

---

* *Not My Will: How Much Will Surrender Cost* (Chicago: Moody Publishers, 2002).

in campus activities, cultivate friendships, or think about God. Eleanor is seeking peace and happiness in diligent work and self-denial. She meets and marries Chad, a Christian student at the university, and is temporarily happy. But Chad dies and, driven by grief and despair, Eleanor plunges deeper into her work in an effort to fill the gap left by Chad's death. Her efforts fail; her grades drop; and she becomes seriously ill.

In the midst of her illness, Eleanor finally realizes that her quest for peace is in vain until she surrenders her life completely to Jesus Christ. Only then does she realize the strength, courage, and comfort that Christ provides when one does His will. After regaining her health, Eleanor feels that God is leading her to finish college. She goes to a Christian college and there earns her degree. Happy and content at last, Eleanor marries a fine Christian preacher and goes into Christian service in the inner city.

Conclusion The author's purpose is to show how a person's struggle for personal independence can lead to frustration. God demands more from us than our struggle for personal peace and prosperity; we are to seek to glorify Him in all we do. Only then can we find fulfillment.

Evaluation Not My Will is an inspiring and moving book. It is enjoyable and profitable reading for anyone. It has shown me how useless it is to try to manage my own life to please myself. Only through surrender to the Lord's will can I have peace and joy. As Eleanor had to give in to God, so must every Christian in order to reap the full benefits of life in Christ. Not My Will is a fine book with a message that will move any reader.

CHAPTER FOUR
IMPROVING YOUR RESEARCH SKILLS:

HOW TO PREPARE A TERM PAPER

Writing a term paper, or research report, is much like a sculptor who takes a massive block of wood or stone, and chisels the material into an original work of art. Likewise, you sculpt a massive block of information into your own creation. A term paper deals with a limited topic and is based on information from books, magazines, and possibly interviews with experts in a particular area of knowledge. Consequently, a research report involves discovering what the experts have to say about any given subject, providing your own analysis of the information you collect, and expressing the opinions you form in the process.

Your term paper should be about four or five typed pages (approximately 2,000 words), or the specified length in your course requirements. You should gather information from at least six sources—one of which should be the encyclopedia. Some sources may prove unsuitable as your research progresses, so identify up to ten sources at the outset in case some are eliminated along the way. Many previously learned skills such as sentence clarity, paragraph building, outline structuring, and theme development apply to the writing of a term paper—but on a grand scale. This report will express your thoughts by description, narration, exposition, or persuasion. Use the following steps in preparing your term paper:

1. **Select** and **limit your topic.**
2. Carry out your **initial library research.** Gather your resources and prepare a working bibliography.
3. Determine your *purpose*, *audience*, and *limiting ideas*.
4. Prepare a **general outline.**
5. Do **detailed library research** by reading and taking notes. (If necessary, revise your initial outline.)
6. Prepare a **detailed outline** from your note cards.
7. Write your **first draft.**
8. Do **additional research** if necessary.
9. Edit and write your **second draft.**
10. **Type the paper** and trial footnotes.
11. Check spelling and **proofread** your work. (Have someone else proofread your paper, if at all possible.)
12. Produce the **final draft**, making any last-minute changes.

Not all papers require the same amount of attention. You must learn to *prioritize your writing assignments*, giving the most important ones the greatest effort. The length of your assigned papers will also determine which ones you tackle first. Of course, if you have been given a five-page project on some obscure subject, you may find it will take you as much time to write as a twenty-page paper on a common topic. In either case, you need to *schedule your time to meet the deadline*. Usually your instructor will give you a list of requirements: topic, purpose, and length of the report; whether footnotes and a bibliography are needed, and how many sources are required; if the paper is to be typed, copied, or hand-written; whether the topic has to be approved; whether an outline and note cards need to be handed in; and if there is any penalty for submitting a late paper. Consequently, *you must plan ahead*.

Photocopy and use the following procedures to guide you in mapping out what you have to do and when:

- Contact a typist by _____. (Do not wait until the last minute, or you may not find someone to help you out.)
- Select your subject by _____.
- Do initial research to limit your subject by _____.
- Scrap your first attempts at choosing a subject, if they are too broad, vague, or abstruse by _____.
- Gather all your research material by _____.
- Create your first draft by _____.
- Lay aside your work for at least one 24-hour period.
- Read your first attempt, making any notes on the draft in regard to additions or deletions by _____.
- Compose your second draft by _____.
- Lay your paper aside for another 24 hours.
- Read your second draft out loud, or have a relative or friend do so for you, by _____.
- Make any final changes. Check sentences for clarity, transitions for effectiveness, grammar, mechanics, and spelling by _____.
- Compose the final draft by _____.
- Proofread by _____.
- Type the final draft by _____.
- Proofread by _____.
- Type the "Works Cited" page or "Selected Bibliography" by _____.
- Submit paper by _____.

These steps may be altered or skipped over, depending on your expertise. You may also save time by typing your own paper. Writing a good paper takes time, so plan ahead. Get out your calendar or long-term schedule and fill in the dates for each step of the process. As a rule of thumb, plan to spend half of your time on **research**, and the other half on **writing**. Let us say your term paper is due in eight weeks, so set aside the first week to choose a subject and decide the approach you want to take. The second week is used to find various sources, and to prepare a bibliography. The third and fourth weeks are reserved for the preliminary outline, reading your references, and taking notes. Be sure to block out two or more hours at fixed times during the week to work on your paper. The fifth and sixth weeks are set apart for detailing your outline and writing the first draft. Week seven should be scheduled for editing and rewriting your work, and preparing your bibliography. When all is said and done, the eighth week is for proofreading and typing the final copy. To begin with, let us take a closer look at your most important research tool—your local library.

1. Using the Library

The library is one of the greatest depositories of human knowledge on this planet. You can also access any type and amount of information that is available in the English language, and more. In your desire to improve your study habits, the library stands out as one of the unsurpassed sources for research and development in almost every subject imaginable. There are more than 123,000 libraries (public, academic, school, military, and government) nationwide,* which not only have a fixed set of volumes, but many provide inter-library loan services on a wide basis. And all this is available for no money down and no interest for the lifetime of the service.

Let us say you have never darkened the door of your local library, and you do not have the foggiest idea where to go to get a book, or how to start your research paper that has been assigned. After locating the library through a local directory, call to make sure of the directions and find out their regular and holiday hours—which vary widely from place to place. Upon entering the library, you may ask someone at the front desk to help you get acquainted with your particular facility. The librarian is a specialist in the area of library science, and can be an immense help in guiding you through the labyrinth of library research and usage. If this valuable resource person is not available, look specifically for the card catalog.

* This statistic is based on data from the American Library Association website (<http://www.ala.org/ala/aboutala/offices/library/libraryfactsheet/alalibraryfactsheet1.cfm>).

A. The Card Catalog & Melvil Dewey

The card catalog was traditionally housed in a large file-type cabinet, listing all the books available at your particular facility. However, today nearly all libraries have replaced the old card catalog system of accessing information with the computer terminal—most systems are online now. In either case, there are three basic ways to locate a specific listing: by title, by author, or by subject. If it is a **fiction** book, then search for it by title or author; but if it is a **non-fiction** book, then look it up by title, author, or subject. All of these titles, authors, and subjects are listed in alphabetical order.

For example, if you have been assigned to read a book by Charles Dickens, simply look under "D" in the card catalog for Dickens. Or if you want to increase your knowledge on insects, look under that topic in the card catalog. Then you can access the books listed by the **call number** or "Dewey decimal number" that is usually located in the upper left-hand corner of the cards in the card catalog. These call numbers were devised by Melvil Dewey, who was born in 1851 and later became a famous librarian and educator. He is best known for originating this system for classifying library books, which is named in his honor. The **Dewey Decimal System** is based on three-digit numbers—as shown in the following table; these numbers are further extended beyond the decimal point for the various subclasses of books. Normally the library is divided up into sections according to these topics devised by Dewey. With the title and call number in hand, look for the corresponding section as follows:

The Dewey Decimal System

000-099	General Reference Works (encyclopedias, dictionaries, indexes, etc.)
100-199	Philosophy (books on how to think)
200-299	Religion (books on the various world religions)
300-399	Social Sciences (government, economics, geography)
400-499	Language Arts (grammar, etymology, foreign languages)
500-599	Science (astronomy, biology, chemistry, etc.)
600-699	Technology (engineering, medicine, etc.)
700-799	Fine Arts (music, painting, theater, sports, etc.)
800-899	Literature (essays, plays, poetry, prose, etc.)
900-999	History (biography, history, and travel)

Figure 4.1

These classifications are basically for non-fiction type books. However, all fiction books are listed under *Literature* in the Dewey decimal system—in alphabetical order by the last name of the author—usually without a number like the other listings. Each of these major headings are then divided further into sub-levels for more limited subjects, and then subdivisions for specific categories under each subject.

The Library of Congress—which is considered the largest library in the world—offers an alternate classification system based on letters, rather than numbers, for major topics. Although this system has greater flexibility than the Dewey decimal system, it is more complex and lacks the logical decimal features of Dewey's system. The Library of Congress is more suitable for larger libraries in academic and research fields. The general classifications for this system are given below:

Library of Congress System

A	General Works	M	Music
B	Philosophy, Religion	N	Fine Arts
C	Auxiliary Sciences of History	P	Language, Literature
D	Universal History	Q	Science
E-F	American History	R	Medicine
G	Geography, Anthropology	S	Agriculture
H	Social Sciences	T	Technology
J	Political Sciences	U	Military Science
K	Law	V	Naval Science
L	Education	Z	Bibliography

Figure 4.2

Here are the three types of catalog cards found in most libraries—based on the Dewey decimal system. Note that the same book and author are used, but they are listed either by subject, author, or title:

	Meteorology	
SUBJECT CARD	551.5 DeYOU	DeYoung, Donald B. Weather and the Bible
	Baker Book House Grand Rapids, MI: 1992, 162p.	

Figure 4.3

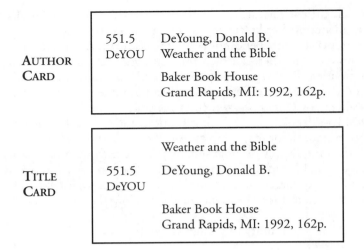

AUTHOR CARD	551.5 DeYOU	DeYoung, Donald B. Weather and the Bible
		Baker Book House Grand Rapids, MI: 1992, 162p.

TITLE CARD		Weather and the Bible
	551.5 DeYOU	DeYoung, Donald B.
		Baker Book House Grand Rapids, MI: 1992, 162p.

Figure 4.4

B. Reference Books and Resources

Besides the books that you are able to check out and take home, there are many **reference books** that can be beneficial to your overall study objectives—although they cannot be removed. The *encyclopedia* is the logical place to start for a general overview of any given topic. This excellent resource provides summary articles, outlines, and sometimes a selected bibliography on a wide range of topics. Other general reference books like dictionaries (e.g., the *Oxford English Dictionary*), thesauri (e.g., *The Synonym Finder*), atlases, handbooks, almanacs, concordances, and other indexes are useful for specific facts and support material in a given area. However, if you desire a more in-depth look, find books in the reference section of the library that contain detailed information on your subject. This is where note-taking skills will be helpful—which will be covered in the next section of this chapter.

Not only should you utilize these reference works, but also magazine and newspaper articles, pamphlets, brochures, government documents, anthologies (collections of poems, stories, excerpts, and so forth—chosen by a compiler), microfilm, film, and video. These are just a portion of the resources that are available for your study and research assignments, found in the reference section of your local library.

C. Reference Indexes and Guides

The best approach to any kind of library research is reviewing a wide variety of sources. But how can you find such a range of reference material on your particular topic? Besides the card catalog, there are several kinds of **indexes** available to you: newspaper and periodical indexes, vertical files, and the *U.S. Documents Monthly Catalog.* The most useful is *The Reader's Guide to Periodical Literature,* which lists published articles from 180 of the most popular magazines in America and Canada. The most recent articles, essays, poems, speeches, and stories will help in giving you the most up-to-date data on your topic. The *Reader's Guide* is published bimonthly, except for the months of February, July, and August when it is done once; all entries are listed by author and subject, except stories, which are listed by title.

The *International Index* is similar, but covers over 250 American and foreign magazines that are more academically oriented. The *Essay and General Literature Index* is also a useful reference tool in locating articles, essays, and speeches found in collected works or compilations. Another often overlooked resource is the association dictionary, which gives any particular organization's historian by name and lists certain specialists in your area of interest. If these experts live close by, you could make a point of interviewing them personally. At least you should write or call them to gain valuable information you would not be able to get any other way. Here are a few easy steps to follow when doing library research:

- Familiarize yourself with your local library.
- Get to know your librarian, who can help you find resources you never dreamed were available.
- Start with the broadest possible topics and outlines, then begin to narrow down your subject to specifics.
- Go first to the dictionary to look up any key words in your topic so you have a clear idea of what you are researching.
- Next, refer to one of the primary encyclopedias such as *Britannica, Americana, Collier's,* or *World Book.* This will give you an overview and historical background on the topic you are researching.
- Consult the *Reader's Guide, Essay Index,* and other principal directories and indexes for more specific information.
- Access the card catalog for books that may be of help in your area of interest.
- Another valuable resource tool is *The Basic Guide to Research Sources,* which lists government and private works, in all areas of knowledge—art, business, education, history, literature, philosophy, mathematics, politics, religion, science, sports, and so forth.
- Remember to make frequent use of your local library because it can become a great "second home."

2. RESEARCHING YOUR TERM PAPER

STEP ONE

Now we are ready to take a closer look at each of the twelve steps for writing a good term paper. Step one involves **selecting** and **limiting your subject**. If you have not been assigned a topic, you should choose one in which you are interested and would like to become an authority. Make sure you have sufficient resource material available, and then begin to limit your subject if it is too broad. Consequently, you will be able to adequately treat it, within the designated number of pages. At this time, write out your purpose or thesis statement. This will help you locate materials and guide your reading.

STEP TWO

Carrying out your **initial library research** is the second step. Read a short background article or encyclopedia entry about the topic. Then choose five to ten sources, which will lead to your preparation of a working bibliography. To begin, skim your library's card catalog, the *Reader's Guide to Periodic Literature*, or other publication indexes, to discover books, magazines, or journal articles that have been written on your subject. Also check the *Essay and General Literature Index* to find essays, articles, and speeches contained in collected works. To locate additional sources that you may not otherwise come across, consult a bibliography of bibliographies—a list of sources of information on all the various fields of knowledge. Make a card* for every source that looks promising while you are compiling your bibliography. Fill each card out completely and accurately the first time, so you do not waste time retracing your steps. Evaluate each source that you have located, using the following steps for your assessment:

a. Determine if the author is well qualified on your subject, and note if the publisher is also a reliable source. Check the date of the work to see if there is any significance to it. Then decide whether or not the book pertains to your topic.

b. You may want to consult an index like the *Book Review Digest* to help you evaluate the reliability of the source. The *Book Review Digest* lists book reviews that are contained in a variety of periodicals and journals. Each entry holds excerpts from as many reviews as are necessary to give a balance of various opinions.

c. At the bottom of each card, jot down a reminder so you will be able to recall the value of that particular source. (Note: on the three-by-five card record the source's location, if necessary. Each card should be numbered in the upper right-hand corner—see page 60.)

* You may use electronic note-taking software or pen tablet for this step, as well.

d. Remove any source cards that are definitely inferior or unrelated to your purpose. Consequently, you will be narrowing your sources to the five or six. These sources will be used in limiting your purpose and ideas that will control your research and writing.

STEP THREE

Step three deals with your *purpose, audience*, and *ideas* that will limit or control your work. Here is where you develop your tentative **purpose** statement—the central argument that will attempt to prove or disprove the main body of your paper. This statement is tentative because it may not wind up being your final purpose. As you progress in the research process, you will be able to focus on a more accurate statement. Often you will be required to submit your purpose statement to your teacher, who will give the kind of feedback you need to help you keep your purpose on target. After you have defined your purpose, you should determine what **audience** you want to address. Your audience will influence how much detail and information you need to include.

Next, crystallize in your mind the **limiting ideas** or thesis statement, which is the central thought that you want to develop in your term paper. State the limiting ideas in a single, precise sentence. Remember, your thesis statement of limiting ideas performs three important functions: (1) expresses the main point of the report, (2) explains to your reader your attitude toward the topic, and (3) proposes the path that your report will follow. In effect, this will help you focus on your purpose—locating appropriate materials and guiding your reading.

STEP FOUR

Step four involves your **general outline**. Give some thought as to how you might approach the subject in your paper, by jotting down various ideas you plan to investigate. After listing the ideas you think should be addressed, eliminate any ideas that are not related to your statement of purpose (or thesis). Group your ideas under several main headings and make the preliminary outline, which will probably include only main headings and subheadings. You should make as many changes as necessary to this general outline while you are taking notes. Insert new topics and remove those that are not essential. This outline will require considerable change before you will be able to base your paper on it.

STEP FIVE

Step five tackles your **detailed library research**—*reading* and *taking notes*. This is where you will spend the bulk of your time, using blank index cards (or electronic software or pen tablet) to write out one thought, idea, quote, or fact per card. In the upper right-hand corner, write the number of the source designated on the bibliography cards you made earlier. The heading for each card should be placed in the upper left-hand corner of the card for easy reading; these headings come from your preliminary outline to which the note pertains. Use a separate card for each note, trying not to carry over a note onto a second card. Record the page number(s) of your source in the lower right-hand corner.

Here are samples of a bibliography card and a note card, that you might use when researching your topic:

Bibliography Card for a Book

AUTHOR	DeYoung, Donald B. 1
TITLE	<u>Weather and the Bible</u>
PUBLICATION INFORMATION	Grand Rapids, MI: 1992 Baker Book House
CALL NUMBER	551.5 DeYOU
NOTATION	Good Source for climate in Israel

Figure 4.5

Note Card on Research Topic

HEADING & SOURCE NUMBER (Note: #1 in upper right-hand corner—corresponds to #1 on bibliography card.) **PAGE NUMBERS**	Cause of Storms 1 **Sect. 66. Storms on Sea of Galilee** sea lies 680 feet below sea level & surrounded by hills—2,000 feet high; cool dry air is funneled by the hills into warm, moist air of the sea; strong winds are created by descending cool air on the lake causing violent results—without warning. pp.99–100

Figure 4.6

A. Reading Research Material

While you are reading and taking notes, be aware of what the *pre-suppositions* (or underlying belief systems) are of writers and the publishers you are consulting. Many writers and even the publishers do not put much confidence in the Bible. You must constantly ask yourself, "Is it in line with the Word of God?" (Proverbs 3:5-7 and Psalm 119:128). Therefore, if a statement contradicts the Bible, it is *not* correct—no matter what others may say! Be cautious, not only of these writers and publishers who reject God's revealed truth in Scripture, but also of so-called Christians who accept human ideas uncritically. Such writers are not trustworthy because they have mixed Christian ideas with man's reasoning. In essence, their writings have not been held up to the high standard of the Bible; therefore, they are suspect.

Furthermore, some writers are fond of saying, "Studies have shown such and such to be factual." Do not be misled or swayed by these pronouncements because they frequently show no such thing. The results of many studies are either erroneous, misleading, or have not been interpreted properly. Especially be wary of certain sociological or psychological studies that state findings based on so-called research that supposedly supports their arguments. Above all, remember that everything you read must pass through the "filter" of God's Word.

B. Note Taking on Research Material

In addition, as you **take notes** you should either summarize, paraphrase, or quote directly from your sources. However, any and all of these ideas must be footnoted when they appear in your paper. Failure to give credit, where credit is due, is called *plagiarism*—the act of taking ideas or writings of someone else and passing them off as your own. Even if you paraphrase or summarize the author's words, you have to footnote your source to avoid plagiarism. This word literally means "the act of kidnapping." In other words, you would be stealing the "brain-child" of another person, which is a serious offense that you should avoid at all cost.

If you choose to summarize or paraphrase most of your notes, your paper will flow easily. However, if you decide to use several **quotations**, then your work is cut out for you. Always enclose these excerpts within quotations marks. Make sure that you copy the quotation accurately, following all punctuation, capitalization, and exact spelling as it appears in your source. At times you may want to omit certain words from a quotation that do not bear directly on your purpose or thesis statement. Use dots or *ellipsis points* to indicate that these words have been omitted. Three dots (...) are used within a sentence to show an omission, while four dots (....) are used for the last part of a sentence, the first part of the next sentence, or a whole sentence or paragraph that has been deleted.

As you move forward in your research, you will become more familiar with your subject. At this point you may want to make some changes. As you take notes, you will want to incorporate or delete certain ideas on your outline. You may also come to realize that your purpose (or thesis) statement does not reflect a true picture of reality. You want to reveal the truth about your subject, so do not hesitate to make those necessary changes. Furthermore, you must stop at times and sort through your cards, placing each note under its proper heading. In this way you will be able to determine areas you may have neglected or overemphasized; then you can make the proper adjustments.

STEP SIX

By step six you will be ready to prepare a **detailed outline** from your note cards. After you have established the accuracy of your preliminary or general outline, make sure that the points are in the best order. You want your work to flow logically, so orderliness is a vital aspect of the research process that will pay dividends in the writing phase of your project. After you have placed your note cards in the right sequence, take a few moments to read through them from front to back. This will become the sketchy draft of your paper. Now you are ready to create your detailed outline that will present your ideas in a logical order.

3. WRITING YOUR TERM PAPER

STEP SEVEN

The **first draft** of your term paper is step seven, which is the next major phase of the research process. This step may be easier than you might think. If you have taken good notes, organized them properly, and developed a well-organized outline, then your first draft will flow quite easily. This process, however, takes peace and quiet—so look for that choice spot that will make your writing a pleasure.

Writing demands concentration and much thought, so find a large enough work space that is free of all distractions. Your desk or table should be well lit, so you can easily read your note cards and write your rough draft. If at all possible, use a computer because this will aid you when you reach step nine—the revision and editing stage. Remember, write fast and furiously. Get your thoughts down on paper or the computer, and do not forget to identify your sources. Do not worry about finding the right word, using the correct grammar, or placing the proper punctuation. All those concerns will come later.

STEP EIGHT

Step eight involves **additional research**. After the first draft is completed, you may realize that some points do not quite fit, or information is lacking under a certain heading. Here you must return to the library or your sources at hand.

STEP NINE

Step nine will take some time because you are ready for the **second draft**. Initially you want to improve the flow of your paper, organize your thoughts better, clarify foggy concepts, and strengthen weak arguments. You need to focus on any problem areas and make editorial changes as you deem necessary. Ask yourself if your paper is complete and in good order. You should check for *oneness, cohesion*, and the proper *stress*. Continue to rewrite each section of your paper until these elements have been satisfied. Subsequently, check each word, phrase, sentence, and paragraph for accuracy and truthfulness. Now you need to examine the grammar and mechanics used in your paper.

STEP TEN

A. Typing Your Term Paper

Step ten is for **typing** your last draft. If you have not had access to a computer previously, now is the time to submit your paper to a typist; or perhaps you plan to type it yourself. In either case, you should use white, twenty-pound, $8\frac{1}{2}$-by-11-inch paper (erasable bond and onion skin types of paper are not acceptable). Do not use any "script" or fancy type styles, which are hard to read and, therefore, inappropriate for this kind of work. In addition, a good cartridge in your printer goes a long way to producing a sharp, clean report. By all means, do not submit your paper with any inserted lines, strikeovers, or crossed-out letters. Corrections done on a personal computer can easily be made prior to your paper being printed.

B. Arranging Your Term Paper

The **layout of your paper** can get quite involved, so you should refer to the style specified by your instructor. This style should be used throughout the paper—styles should NOT be mixed. We recommend *Writing a Research Paper* (published by Christian Liberty Press, 1998), which is based on the **Modern Language Association** (MLA) **style**. Also, Kate L. Turabian's *A Manual for Writers of Term Papers, Theses, and Dissertations* (7th ed.; Chicago, IL: University of Chicago Press, 2007) is an extremely popular manual, which has historically been the standard for many universities and publishers; it is known as the **Chicago**

style. In addition, James A. Chapman's *Handbook of Grammar and Composition* (4ᵗʰ ed.; Pensacola, FL: A Beka Book Publications, 2006) has a thorough, concise section on writing a research report; Chapman's *Handbook* incorporates the Chicago style.

Basically, you need a title page, outline page(s), and then the body of the paper. After this, you should work on possible appendices, text notes (footnotes, endnotes, or parenthetical notes), and finally a list of sources (a "Works Cited" or bibliography page). Refer to *Writing a Research Paper* for the MLA style (i.e., when using parenthetical notes and a "Works Cited" page) or Turabian's *Manual* for the Chicago style (i.e., when using footnotes and a bibliography)—both offer insight on any technical questions you might face. *Remember not to mix styles*.

Usually the first page of your paper should contain the title of your paper, centered on the twelfth line down from the top of the page. The rest of the paper should use standard margins and spacing between sentences, paragraphs, and headings. Double-space the text, and center Arabic numerals on the fifth line from the bottom of the page for numbering subsequent pages. Start typing on the seventh line from the top of the page, for all pages after the first one. For block quotations check *Writing a Research Paper* or Turabian's *Manual* for the proper format, consistently following your assigned style (MLA or Chicago).

C. Referencing Your Term Paper

Text notes, or source citations, are an important aspect of a well-documented paper. Word processing software makes this step easy. One type of text notes is **footnotes**, which need to be typed prior to the final draft for spacing purposes at the bottom of each page. These are single-spaced and indented eight spaces from the left margin. Double-space between footnotes that follow one after another. It is proper to place a number slightly above the line for each footnote (or use the superscript function on your computer), which refers back to the paraphrase or direct quote mentioned in the body of the paper. This number is also used within the text, raised slightly above the line at the end of the material cited. *Footnotes should be numbered consecutively* throughout your paper, starting with the number one (1). Place each corresponding footnote at the bottom of the same page. Remember to use the shortened format for all references to sources already cited earlier in your paper; if they are short enough, place them in a line using three spaces between each. Always leave room for the page number, which is five spaces from the bottom, and a single space below the last footnote.

Perhaps you may decide to use **endnotes**, which would come at the end of your paper—before the bibliography. Basically, each entry follows the basic form of a footnote. When using endnotes, be sure to consult Turabian or Chapman for the proper format. One advantage of endnotes is that the length of each note is not a problem—allowing you to make additional comments, as necessary. However, one disadvantage is that you need to put all the necessary information down in the note, even if it was mentioned in the text.

Since 1988 the Modern Language Association has recommended the use of **parenthetical notes** instead of the use of footnotes or endnotes; therefore, the MLA style has become the standard for many colleges and universities and is the standard for the Christian Liberty Academy School System (refer to *Writing a Research Paper*). Parenthetical notes are descriptions placed within the body of your paper, acknowledging the source of your information. Since parenthetical notes are very brief, a "Works Cited" page is prepared and placed at the end of the paper. This page gives a more detailed description of the sources used.

D. Listing References Used in Your Paper

Finally, you come to your "Works Cited" or bibliography page, which lists only the sources quoted or referred to in your paper. This alphabetized list is called "WORKS CITED" for the MLA style or "SELECTED BIBLIOGRAPHY" for the Chicago style, and should be titled in this manner. If you arrange your bibliographic citation cards in alphabetical order, this process will go quickly. Use the first word that appears on the note card. This will usually be the author's last name, or the first word in the title of the source, except for *a*, *an*, and *the*. Between the title and first line of the citations you should use triple-spacing. Each entry should be singled-spaced, and then between entries use double-spacing. In contrast to indented footnotes, the line of each entry of a bibliography is flush with the left margin, and subsequent lines are indented eight spaces. Right-handed margins, numbering of pages, and the following pages of the bibliography conform to the guidelines used in the body of the text.

STEP ELEVEN

Step eleven covers the final check of spelling and proofreading of your work. Do not carelessly skip this important step. Glaring mistakes in spelling, grammar, or punctuation do not reflect well on your abilities, nor do they benefit your final grade. Consult your dictionary, thesaurus, grammar handbook, or any other reference that will help in the process of checking for errors. Carefully examine each typed page with your original manuscript to see if any portion was overlooked. Proofread every word, phrase, sentence, and paragraph for proper usage: spelling, clarity, oneness, cohesion, stress, order, grammar, and mechanics. Remember, *you* will be held accountable for the final product, *not* your typist.

Therefore, you must take the proper measures, regardless of the cost or pain, to scrutinize every letter, mark, and word so no errors will slip by. It is best to *seek out a good proofreader* such as a parent, relative, or friend who can go over your paper—easily spotting certain things you have missed. The fact is, you are so close to the report that you cannot see these inaccuracies.

STEP TWELVE

The twelfth step involves incorporating any changes your proofreader has suggested. After this, you will be able to **type the final draft**. Then go over your report again—carefully! This is sometimes referred to as the *publication stage* because you are in essence offering your work to the public. Normally you begin your paper with a title page that contains the title, your name, your instructor's name, the course name and number, and the due date. Proofread your final draft at least twice for any errors, and make the necessary changes. Perhaps you may want to go to a local copyshop or printer to have your paper finalized.

It always pays to have some kind of backup copy in case the original is lost or damaged. Now you are ready to submit your manuscript!

CHAPTER FIVE

IMPROVING YOUR STUDY HABITS

You want to improve the way you study, but where do you begin? You may have come to realize that *studying* is a fact of life. Last minute attempts at cramming for a test or writing a paper have not been as profitable as you thought. So you long for some workable approach to the inevitable. Obviously, studying involves certain habits and techniques that will help in the following areas: the use of the library, taking notes, listening to others, reading a textbook, and studying history, mathematics, and science. But you need to know where to begin the "race"—determining what habits or skills you must focus in on. You have to identify the areas in which you are weak, clarify those subjects that you enjoy, and then determine how well you do in each of them.

SELF-EVALUATION
Honestly evaluate your ability in these ten areas:
- Time management
- Reading aptitude
- Writing skills
- Composition skills
- Library skills
- Taking notes
- Listening skills
- Preparation for an exam
- Taking a test
- Memorizing material

Initially, rate yourself on a scale of 1 to 10—where 10 is the best—in each area; then set aside some time to test yourself accordingly. Perhaps your parents or instructor can help you do this exercise. In the area of *time management*, ask yourself, "Do I normally break down each of my assignments into individual steps, and complete them on time?" If you already use a long-term schedule, and a short-term weekly schedule for your more immediate tasks, then give yourself a high mark. In the area of *reading aptitude*, test how fast you read and how much you comprehend by taking a short passage and reading it for speed and understanding. Then check the time it took (words per minute), and jot down how much you remembered (rereading the passage for what you may have missed).

For *writing* and *composition*, refer back to your past work to evaluate your skills in these areas. Honestly appraise your abilities. In the area of *library usage*, ask yourself, "Have I used the library within the last month, or has it been awhile?", "Do I know my way around the library—where the reference area is, or how the Dewey decimal system works?" If you have gone to your local library recently, and know how to find the information or books you need, give yourself a high mark. Likewise, create different ways of testing yourself in the rest of these areas, and score yourself accordingly. If you have a combined score of 90 to 100, give yourself an A; if you received 70 to 89 points, give yourself a B; if you scored 70 to 79, give yourself a C; but if you earned 69 or less, you need to improve significantly in one or more areas.

MOTIVATION

Now that you have completed your self-evaluation, you can focus on the areas in which you need to improve. But first we should look at your *motivations*—why you do what you do. Usually you are interested in a particular course or subject, so you find it easier to dig in and learn. However, that is not always the case with each class you take. Therefore, you must seek some outside incentive for studying material that does not come easily to you. Perhaps you are motivated to study a particular subject because it is required for graduation, which may be enough to prompt you to do the necessary work. But the best motivation is a desire to glorify God in all that you do (1 Corinthians 10:31).

GOAL SETTING

However, aiming toward a long-term goal—what you would like to be doing five to ten years from now—would give you more incentive to learn. Visualize what type of work or profession you would like to enter and the kinds of activities that would entail. If you do not have a goal to aim for, it is hard to reach it. So work toward a clear goal; then you will be able to arrange your educational goals around the goals you have set for your career.

Setting goals should become a regular part of your lifestyle, realizing that good study habits will help you achieve them. To make goal setting part of your life, you have to be realistic. Do not aim too high—you may get bogged down with too much work. Do not aim too low—you may not be challenged with respect to your abilities. Your expectations should be *reasonable*, so do not seek mastery in a subject in which you have little interest or ability. It is better to gain some knowledge in the course, rather than becoming discouraged and giving up. You need to be *flexible*—adjusting your goals as you progress by increasing your expectations in one area and decreasing your work load in another.

FOCUSING

Concentrate on the areas where you know you will undoubtedly succeed because success in any given subject will give you the boost you need to keep going. Building your confidence will go a long way to keeping you on track and helping you to accomplish more than you ever imagined. By all means, review your goals on a regular basis, and make the necessary adjustments on your daily schedule, short-term, and long-term goals. And do not forget to reward yourself for a job well done—and done on time.

We have already covered where your studying should take place under the "Let's Get Started" section. But it is noteworthy to mention again the need to have a good work area that is well lit and free of any distractions. You also need to be rested and in fairly good health to do your best. Moreover, determine the best time for you to get the task at hand accomplished, as well as how often you need to take a break. All of these aspects of studying should be determined before you begin studying. Now we are ready to begin, so let us start with note taking.

1. TAKING NOTES

Learning how to *take good notes* is an important skill that will pay dividends in the long run. As you study, you can help your retention level by jotting down those points that you deem significant. A short, concise sentence or phrase will help you recall the main idea of each paragraph. In subjects such as Bible, geography, history, and even certain science texts, select key sentences and rewrite them in your own words. As you develop your note-taking skills, you will notice a marked improvement in your school work. In fact, you will begin to enjoy your studies more as you grasp the overall picture of your course work. Note taking ultimately focuses your reading, which helps you to stay on track—minimizing any and all distractions.

A. Thinking While Taking Notes

Obviously, you should obtain the right tools for taking notes—pen, three-ring binder, and notebook paper. But the most crucial instrument you need is an *active mind*. You must decide to get involved with the material in front of you. It does not matter if you are listening to someone speak or if you are reading a textbook, your brain must be engaged as you take notes. A large part of this skill has to do with listening—especially if you are sitting in a classroom or attending a lecture. Whether or not the lecturer is speaking slowly, your brain actually functions at a greater speed than anyone can speak. So to prevent your mind from wandering, keep your brain engaged by taking notes.

B. Listening While Taking Notes

The next couple of paragraphs deal with a formal classroom setting. Even though this may not apply to you directly, the ideas expressed here will enhance your future studies in college and beyond. To begin with, you should *maintain eye contact* with the lecturer at all times. Wandering eyes can be your downfall, especially if you have the desire to learn and apply the knowledge being presented. You also need to *concentrate* on what the speaker is saying and not try to formulate what you want to say in response. This is not only antiproductive, it is impolite. In addition, you should develop the habit of *asking questions* on a frequent basis. This will keep you attentive and the lecturer on the alert. These are all excellent techniques to help you improve your listening and note-taking skills.

Make it a goal to eliminate as many distractions as possible. *Sit near the front of the room*, where you can hear and see better. When people sit in front of you, the speaker may be out of your line of vision and your thoughts may tend to wander. People in front of you are also inclined to be more interesting than the person speaking—their quirks, idiosyncrasies, and personal hygiene are all possible distractions. Sitting near the speaker is the best place to be because you can understand what is being said, and you can ask and answer questions more easily. *Sit up straight*, to help you in the listening and note-taking process. Since poor posture can bring on aches and pains you never knew possible, you should straighten up and get comfortable.

Also, do not get sidetracked by *recording lectures* you plan to attend. It is very time consuming to listen twice to the lecture, not to mention rewinding the recording back and forth to find the information you need. Listening and taking notes at the outset is better than depending on a device that might malfunction or a tape that may get jammed. Moreover, the cost of a pen and paper is minuscule in comparison with a good digital recorder, reliable batteries, and quality tapes. Of course, if the lecture is of a technical nature, a voice recorder may come in handy; but nothing substitutes for good listening and note-taking skills.

Here are seven ways you can improve your note-taking skills through listening:

1. **Develop an active mind.** Do not just sit there, but interact with the material.
2. **Maintain eye contact.** Do not let your eyes wander, or you may get sidetracked.
3. **Concentrate on what is being said** by the speaker—not on what you want to say in response.

4. **Ask questions frequently.** In this way you can gain insight and stay attentive.
5. **Sit near the front.** Often people in front of you will draw your attention away from the speaker.
6. **Sit up straight.** Poor posture can cause distracting aches and pains, so sit erect.
7. **Avoid recording lectures.** This can become time consuming and costly. Use this technique only under certain circumstances.

C. Note Taking for the Classroom

There are basically *two approaches to taking notes* that will help you become a more successful student. The first kind deals with **note taking for the classroom**, which may not apply directly to homeschoolers now, but it will pay dividends in the future—undergraduate and graduate studies, lectures, seminars, and conferences—not to mention Sunday morning sermons. A *three-ring binder* is essential because you can add, subtract, or switch a page here and there without much difficulty. You also can insert supplemental material (handouts, quizzes, copies of articles from magazines, and homework assignments) easily when and where it is needed—with the help of a three-hole punch. In addition, you can reorganize your notes faster if the instructor amplifies a topic from an earlier lecture. A subsequent feature to using a three-ring binder is portability—you can leave it at home and just take a lightweight folder with a few sheets of paper and a pen to class.

The next thing to do is to **listen** before you begin to write. Some fall into the trap of trying to copy down every word they hear the teacher utter. However, if your mind is actively digesting the material that is being presented, then you will be able to *paraphrase* and **enter what is essential** into your notes. You should seek to acquire an overall picture of the lecturer's main thrust. Do not get bogged down with numerous details and dates that can be referred to later in your textbook. Also, pass over information you already know, especially if it is being used to clarify a particular point. Undoubtedly, different types of classes demand different kinds of note taking: straight lectures require extensive notes; tutorials and discussion groups are interactive, so they call for fewer notes; and science, language, and art labs provide more hands-on opportunities, and may or may not demand many notes.

Most of all, be aware that every teacher has a particular **plan of attack** for each lecture. You should attempt to learn and follow this strategy early on. In this way your note taking will help you focus on what the teacher actually expects from you, as revealed by the exams that he gives, and not necessarily everything that is said in class. But normally a good teacher follows an assigned text, upon which he either expands or clarifies. Read ahead and complete assigned material, so you can understand what is being covered each day. This will strengthen your participation in class. Finally, read over your notes immediately after the class is finished, whenever possible. This will help you to fill in those missing pieces that you did not have time to write down and to reinforce the lesson material.

D. Note Taking for Assigned Reading

The second approach has to do with **note taking for assigned reading**. You will be able to glean many ideas already learned from taking notes in a classroom setting and transfer them to this kind of note taking. First you must read, next you should grasp the "big picture," and *then* begin to write down your notes on what you have discovered. Initially, you should check the title page, the table of contents, and the basic structure of your textbook. Look for the hints the author gives along the way—chapter headings, subheadings, end-of-chapter reviews, pictures, charts, graphs, italicized or boldface words and phrases, highlighted portions, and the question sections.

Going over the **general outline of the book** and skimming over the chapter summaries can go a long way in developing an overall perspective of what the author is emphasizing. Many texts also have maps, tables, diagrams, and illustrations that will enhance your understanding of the material and capsulize difficult concepts that cannot be easily depicted in words. Highlighted portions, italicized words or phrases, and boldface terms are used to bring your attention to key ideas that the writer is trying to emphasize. Finally, do not overlook the questions set forth by the author at the end of each chapter or section division, which stress the main points of the text. Upon completing these preliminary steps, the actual reading of the text will move along more quickly than you originally planned. Rather than having to reread the text because you rushed through it earlier, begin by reading slowly enough so you can grasp the material. The best way to read is not with speed, but with *comprehension*.

Taking good notes does take effort, but not necessarily much time. As the old adage goes, you should *work smarter, not harder*. Careful reading and good note taking are crucial in consistently earning the best grades. The goal is to **organize the important points** from the text in such a way that you can easily understand the material at a glance, increase your retention of the material's content, and prepare for your exams with efficiency. Do not write out complete sentences when you take notes. Capture the principal ideas in key phrases; then place the most important supporting details under them.

When you are ready to jot down your findings, set up a set of terms or letters that represent key individuals in the material being discussed, or major concepts that you can easily identify upon returning to your notes at a later date. Then make a **rough outline** of the article or section, leaving space so you can fill in the missing details as you "dig" further. To make concise, useful notes—ask the following questions:

- What are the most important points that have emerged while I was reading?
- What information must I look for that will be covered on the next exam?
- What are the important theories or concepts from other sources that are explained or expanded on in this article?

One of the best ways to organize your thoughts is by developing a **detailed outline**. So before you start taking notes, spend some time making an outline of the material you need to cover. This will help you review the text more easily and will give your memory "handles" on which to grab—helping you to recall what has been read previously. A side benefit of outlining is the ability to see how a writer's mind works—in a logical way. This will help you immensely in your attempts as a budding writer as well. Moreover, some students like to underline or highlight the text, but unfortunately they have to reread each section to grasp what was underscored. You would be better off reconstructing the author's original outline—recreating the logical construction of his thoughts—in your own words. This will emphasize the important points in your thinking, in contrast to the subordinate ones.

A quick review of "Crafting an Outline" in Chapter Two will refresh your memory on how to construct a standard outline. Roman numerals should be used to represent chapter titles, capital letters to indicate sub-headings, and Arabic numerals to mark individual sections. Also look for key transitional expressions such as: *therefore, since, because, thus, in summary*, and so forth. A **glossary of important words** is also necessary in taking good notes because many writers and teachers expect their readers or students, respectively, to understand and use these terms on an exam. Write down any new or difficult words you discover while you are reading; then immediately look them up, or perhaps find out their meaning at a more convenient time. After you have completed your notes, review them by marking the most important items with an asterisk (*) or by highlighting them. Taking notes can be one of the most freeing and rewarding skills you can develop as a student. This skill will boost your comprehension, grades, exam scores, and overall performance.

Consider the following excerpt with the key ideas listed down the left-hand column.

Martin Luther's Ninety-Five Point Thesis

Excerpt from *Streams of Civilization,*
Volume One
(Arlington Heights, IL:
Christian Liberty Press, 1992)
by Mary Stanton and Albert Hyma

Who

Background

A prominent leader in the Protestant break from the Roman Church was Martin Luther. His father was a German copper smelter, who became wealthy by renting equipment to the mines. Martin Luther was studying to be a lawyer at the University of Erfurt. He then changed his mind and became a monk.

Setting

Conflict

Why

Luther taught in the small German town of Wittenburg. This was in the territory of an independent ruler known as the Elector of Saxony. Trouble started when a Dominican friar named Tetzel began selling indulgences. When Luther found out about it, he was angry. Indulgences were contrary to his belief in justification by faith. He believed if people were saved and forgiven for their sins by the blood of Jesus, they did not need indulgences.

Response

Key Date

Result

Luther wrote a thesis of 95 points attacking indulgences and major Church abuses. He then posted it on the Church door in Wittenburg, a practice used by scholars to announce their willingness to debate issues. The day he posted the thesis—October 31, 1517—is sometimes called the birthday of the Protestant Reformation. Martin Luther must have been surprised at the attention his work received. Soon copies of his thesis were translated into foreign languages and spread throughout Europe.

2. READING A NEW TEXTBOOK

Few of us would want to build a house without first consulting a blueprint and obtaining the proper tools. However, we approach reading a new textbook with little or no foresight. If your goal is to *gain knowledge*—as it should be—remember that you cannot gain it by osmosis. With this goal in mind, gather the necessary tools you need to access this information. In other words, it does not happen by chance, but by a plan of action. Listed below are ten steps that will guide you in your pursuit of knowledge:

> Step 1. **Read the title and try to grasp its meaning.**
> Step 2. **Read the reviews and interact with the experts.**
> Step 3. **Read about the author's background.**
> Step 4. **Read the table of contents.**
> Step 5. **Read the preface, foreword, and introduction.**
> Step 6. **Read the chapter summaries.**
> Step 7. **Skim the text and take notes.**
> Step 8. **Read the footnotes or endnotes.**
> Step 9. **Read the book.**
> Step 10. **Summarize the knowledge you gained.**

Before you begin any reading project, you should keep two vital perspectives in the back of your mind—yours and the author's. Obviously, everyone has a particular *worldview* or underlying principles of life by which each of us operates. Even though some may claim they do not have such a perspective, all of us have been influenced over the years by the words and thoughts of others. This influence guides us in the way we think and the decisions we make, whether or not we are conscious of it. Therefore, as Christians we must firmly hold to the underlying principles of Scripture; then we will not be swayed by the unbiblical thinking of godless men.

If we believe that God is sovereign and Jesus Christ is Lord, then all of our activities in life, including reading, will be influenced by this fact. Likewise, as there is order within the Triune Godhead, there is order in God's creation; and this order should permeate the way we think and act. Since our faith is based on the Word of God, His words to us should ultimately be our guide in reading the words of men, protecting us from the "wiles of the devil" (Ephesians 6:11). It is interesting to note that many insist on quoting the Bible while they are witnessing—and rightly so; but if we follow the example of Jesus, we see that He quoted the Scriptures only when confronting the devil or wicked men! Therefore, it behooves us to know and memorize God's Word so we can stand in the day of evil.

Therefore, we must put all the words we read through the "filter" of God's Word. We should discern *the worldview held by the author* before we begin filling our minds with that person's ideas. Ask yourself the following questions: Does this writer believe in the God of the Bible? Does this person view man as lost, in need of the Savior? Does the author believe in the Lordship of Christ? Does this writer hold to the *inerrancy* of Scripture? (If you do not know what "inerrancy" means, now is the time to use your dictionary skills to discover its meaning.) All of us hold some perspective on these vital matters, so it is essential for us to "filter" all that we read through these four questions to keep us mindful of the unbiblical ideas that might creep into our thought patterns and lead us astray. Now we can begin to follow the *ten steps* to reading a textbook.

STEP ONE

The first step is straightforward—reading and understanding the **title**. This is the key that opens the door you are about to enter. Many titles are followed by a **subtitle** that reveals the author's intent. Look for the clues found here and on the dust jacket of the book. This jacket usually contains the main thrust of the author, which further illuminates the meaning of the title and subtitle. If the text is in paperback, the dust jacket will not be included (although some paperbacks now print the information contained in it on the inside front and back covers). In this case, you can go to the library and see if they have a copy of the text with the dust jacket in tact; and then record the data on three-by-five cards. The main thing to look for on the jacket is the endorsements that are usually listed there. Look for respected, well-known writers that you can trust, and find out what they say about the text. Next, notice if the book is recommended by known newspapers, magazines, or organizations in whom you can put your confidence.

STEP TWO

Step two involves a bit of library research. The first place to look is the *Book Review Digest*, which includes brief summaries of larger **reviews** found in periodicals or journals. For more thorough coverage of what others have written about the textbook, go to those periodicals themselves and make photocopies that can be inserted into your three-ring notebook (see the previous section on note taking). Another helpful resource is the *Book Review Index*, which only lists the periodicals that contain the reviews and does not at all attempt to condense them. In addition, there are more journals and periodicals cited in it than those in the *Book Review Digest*.

STEP THREE

The third step encourages you to investigate the **background of the author**. You can gain valuable insights into the text you are about to read by looking into the history of the author, discovering why he decided to write the book in the first place. A helpful resource, called *Contemporary Authors*, is available at your local library, which gives you the author's previous educational experience, what he has published in the past, and what type of work he has engaged in formerly. An added feature in this resource is the "Sidelights" sections, which supply detailed information on the author's philosophy of life or worldview. These kinds of tidbits are excellent morsels to include in an essay-type exam. The insights that you gain will no doubt assist you in comprehending the overall thrust of the text, as well.

STEP FOUR

Step four entails the strategy that the author has used to attack the subject at hand. The **table of contents** is just such a game plan, which outlines the author's approach for you. A good way to keep this plan in mind at all times is to make a copy of it. Stick it in your textbook so you will be able to refer to it on a regular basis. Jot down any important concepts or page numbers in the margin of your copy, and highlight the key chapters or subheadings if they are included. At test time you will already have a ready-made plan of attack of your own.

If you are in a classroom situation, you will have the added input of your teacher, who gives you certain "stratagems" or pointers along the way. After you have completed your initial reading of the text, and have added what your teacher has said, make any needed adjustments to your copy of the table of contents, reflecting more accurately the direction you should take. In this way, you will be able to streamline your study time for an exam by skipping over unimportant material and concentrating on the significant chapters or sections. If you are in a classroom situation, you should note the chapters that the teacher has omitted, and possibly use the content of these portions on an essay-type test to show you have read and comprehended all the material.

STEP FIVE

Step five covers three preliminary devices used to focus in on the author's purpose for writing. First is the **preface**, which contains the reasons why the author wrote the book and sometimes includes the methodology used in researching the subject. Perhaps the writer wants to fill in a gap that he feels has been overlooked by his colleagues in their particular area of study. Another reason for the author writing might be a new development in the field that should be included or placed in a formal context. Maybe a particular idea or conviction has been misconstrued and needs to be addressed in a penetrating review, so the writer has chosen to analyze it thoroughly.

A second device used is the **foreword**, where an eminent person strongly recommends the book and normally brings his or her own unique perspective. Continue to gather these tidbits, as well, so you can get a fuller view of where the author is going to take you. Third, we come to the **introduction**, which is a vital aspect of the text and should definitely be read. This will give you the main thrust of the book in a nutshell and set the scene either through historical background or by the author fully stating his thesis. Therefore, these preliminary devices will give you a complete perspective on what the author is emphasizing and save you time by focusing your attention before you begin to read the text itself.

STEP SIX

The sixth step simply highlights the **chapter summaries**, which explain what has been expanded upon in the chapters as a whole. These summaries can be viewed as "snapshots" of what was covered previously, giving you an overall picture of the contents found in the chapter itself. Use this important tool each time you begin your assigned reading, which will save you a great deal of time. Do not risk the chance of being overwhelmed by the material again. Use the chapter summary to keep you on course.

STEP SEVEN

Step seven consists of **skimming the text** and taking notes. Initially read the book casually, taking brief notes as you go along. This is not the time to scrutinize every last detail, but to leisurely read and to jot down a few key thoughts. The opening paragraphs of the chapter will clarify what the author wants to accomplish in this particular section. If any given portion does not quite fit the main thrust of the book, make a note and include it in your written work or on your exams. It will show that you understand what has been read and can interact with the material. If you own your textbook, jot these concise thoughts down either in the front or back page(s) of the book.

You could probably go to great lengths in the **note-taking process**, but the key is to only *select information* that relates to the course at hand or to an assigned writing project. Upon finishing the book, transfer your thoughts to your three-ring notebook. After you have completed your reading, you will have a better idea of what should be retained. You could look at this as your own book review, which will be to your advantage come test time or when you write a paper.

STEP EIGHT

The eighth step involves reading the **footnotes** or **endnotes**, as the case may be. This is an excellent way to find other resource material because the author cites various works he has either paraphrased or quoted in the text. These notes are normally found at the bottom of the page, but sometimes they appear at the end of the chapter or after the appendices. Occasionally they include some valuable bits of information that may help you in writing a paper or point you to a certain book you may want to add to your library. In any event, do not overlook these valuable comments at the bottom of this page.

STEP NINE

Step nine is what you have been waiting for: **reading the text.** Many often overlook the previous steps and jump right into the textbook, without getting the "big picture." But once you have done this, you can now begin wading through the book, outlining the important points and possibly underlining or highlighting the text. And do not forget your trusty dictionary for those new or difficult words that may hold the key to the unifying thesis of the text. You may even want to insert the meaning of a particular term in the margin next to where it occurs, so you do not have to look it up again later. Furthermore, refer to the author's purpose on a continual basis so you can determine whether or not what you are reading holds true. If not, write it down for later reference.

STEP TEN

Finally, step ten augments what you have read by taking detailed notes within the context of a detailed outline. Now you may think that this whole section on "Reading a New Textbook" is contradictory to what has been stated previously in the "Taking Notes" section. However, now is the time to start the note-taking process—after you have completed reading the book. Go back and review what was stated in the "**Note Taking for Assigned Reading**" section (page 72), which focuses on what you should do here. Basically, you have been reading for the "big picture," so now you should write concise phrases into a rough outline. Upon completing this task, you will be ready to create a detailed outline that will ultimately be your framework for the note-taking process.

3. STUDYING HISTORY AND GOVERNMENT

Studying the various aspects of man's *past* and *present* should help us to understand the world around us, and what the world could be in the *future*. **History** covers what man has done in the past—economically, politically, socially, intellectually, and religiously. To be an intelligent citizen, it behooves us to learn what man has accomplished, or failed to accomplish. All that has happened in the past has made our country, and the world as a whole, what it is today. So it is with the study of the present—**government**, economics, politics, religion, and so forth. It is also necessary for the well-informed person to know and to act on this knowledge—to be the best citizen he or she can possibly be.

You do not learn about history or civics by memorizing facts—although there is a place for that. These facts, however, are a means to an end, rather than an end in and of themselves. Instead of trying to second guess what the questions and answers are going to be on your next exam, strive to *develop an inquisitive mind*. Ask questions *yourself*—Who? What? Where? Why? and How? Do not wait for the exam to do all the asking! And by all means, do not seek to memorize certain facts just for a quiz or test, but try to *understand what is behind the facts*. Here are some helpful suggestions for you to follow so you can benefit from your study of history or government:

• **Develop a sense of time.** It is good to create a time line of some sort, where you can place major events in history. Learn the principal players and important characteristics of each historical period—such as the times of Abraham (2000 B.C.), Moses (1500 B.C.), David (1000 B.C.), Cyrus (500 B.C.), the birth of Jesus Christ (4 B.C.), the Fall of Rome (A.D. 476), the Middle Ages (500 to 1500), the Crusades (1000 to 1200), the Renaissance (1200 to 1500), Martin Luther and the Reformation (1500 to 1600). If you memorize these ten people or events, you will be able to place most other important dates chronologically.

• **Develop a sense of cause-and-effect.** Learn why certain events took place when they did and what causes produced the end results. If a war took place, ask why it started. If a law was decreed, find out why it was given. If a particular country has a certain kind of government, discover how this came about. Cultivate an inquisitive mind!

• **Develop a sense of which facts are important.** As you learn more about each period of time, start to ask yourself pertinent questions, which will help you focus on the important details. Ask *who* are the important players in these particular events. Ask *what* those important events were and *why* they are significant. Ask *when* these important events took place and *how* they fit into the overall time line you have created. Ask *where* these particular events took place.

• **Develop a sense of the geographic backdrop** when studying history or government (or civics, economics, politics, religion, and so forth). The geography of a country is a clue to its past and present. This would include its climate, mountains, rivers, resources, and also its neighbors. Become acquainted with a good atlas, and look up the specific area you are studying on a map. For example, Rand McNally's *Classroom Atlas* has several different kinds of world maps at the front of the book: relief or topographical (showing elevation with respect to sea level), political, economic, population, and climate maps. In addition, the regional maps that follow show various relief, climate, and political data.

Use the following hints to guide you in your study of history and government:

1. Underline or highlight any vital statistics—dates, facts, causes, and effects.
2. Draw or trace a map of the places you are studying. Mark the important information at the proper location on the map.
3. Create a chart or *time line* of the major events that took place—wars, laws passed, regulations laid down, and so forth.
4. Make a list of the important historical terms that relate to the particular time period you are covering.
5. Keep a *three-ring binder* where you can add your outlines, charts, maps, and any subsequent information on your study of history or government.

4. MASTERING THE *SQ3R* METHOD

SURVEY

QUESTION

READ

RECITE

REVIEW

For studying science, biology, algebra, geometry, geography, and other such subjects, the *SQ3R* **method** has been found to be very helpful. This particular method was developed by Dr. Francis P. Robinson in 1964. In his book *Effective Study* he explained these five simple steps: Survey, Question, Read, Recite, and Review—thus *SQ3R*. After you have perused the introductory material such as the preface, foreword, and introduction to your textbook, examine the **table of contents**. This will give you a good *working outline* to build on. Then use the *SQ3R* method to help you understand what you are reading, so that you can either recite or recall the information you need to know for class or on an exam, respectively. Let us take a closer look at each step.

SURVEY – When you begin studying a particular chapter, read through the various headings, which are usually in boldface type—or set off from the rest of the text in some way. This survey of the chapter will let you know the important facts and key ideas found there. Read through the summary paragraph, which contains the same important information, but at the end of the chapter. List these in your three-ring binder so you can easily glance over them—to see the order and overall development of the text. Examine the review questions at the end of the chapter, as well.

Here is an example of a chapter outline found in an algebra textbook (*New Elementary Algebra: Embracing the First Principles of the Science*) written by Charles Davies, LL.D., and published by A. S. Barnes & Company in 1869:

CHAPTER VII
"Square Root. Radicals of the Second Degree."

1. Definitions—Perfect Squares—Rules—Examples
2. Square Root of Fractions
3. Square Root of Monomials
4. Imperfect Squares, or Radicals
5. Addition of Radicals
6. Subtraction of Radicals
7. Multiplication of Radicals
8. Division of Radicals
9. Square Root of Polynomials

QUESTION – After completing the survey step, formulate questions out of the section headings. In this way you will fix the main points of the chapter firmly in your mind. This will take some practice, but eventually you will make a habit out of making questions in this manner. Ask yourself, "What other vital information should I know from this assignment?" Making questions will aid you in connecting this information with what you already know. Subsequently, look at the questions normally provided at the end of the chapter to further help you in this exercise.

The following questions arise from the headings mentioned above, as well as from the content found in the text under each heading:

1. What is the definition of a square root? A perfect square?
   What are the five rules that are required?
2. How can a square root of a fraction be extracted?
   What is the basic rule of extraction?

3. How should the square root of a monomial be found?
   What are the two rules that must be followed?
4. What are imperfect squares or radicals?
   How should these be extracted? And what are the rules?
5. How are radicals added together if they are similar?
   If the radicals are not similar, how are they added?
   What are the two rules that should be remembered?
6. How are radicals subtracted? And what are the rules?
7. How are radicals multiplied? And what are the rules?
8. How are radicals divided? And what are the rules?
9. How should the square root of polynomials be found?
   What are the four rules that need to be followed?

READ – Step three involves finding the answers to these questions. To answer the questions under the first section, read the material under the first heading. In our example, the first one is: "Definitions — Perfect Squares — Rules — Examples." Keep looking for the correct answers until you have discovered them. Reread the section if necessary. Once you are sure of the answer, write it down on a separate piece of paper so it can be inserted later into your three-ring binder.

RECITE – After completing the answers, glance away from your notes and try to answer the questions from memory. If necessary, read the section again until you have mastered the information. When you have recited the answers correctly, go to the next heading and repeat the process: *question*, *read*, and *recite*. Once you have completed all the sections, proceed to the next step.

REVIEW – After you have finished the above steps, you need to review the entire chapter by going over your notes—without consulting your book. When you have gained a comprehensive understanding of the whole assignment, look for the relationships between each of the items. Does the information flow logically? Now check your memory to see if you can recall the main points without your notes, as well. After such a review, you will have a good handle on your assignment.

The *SQ3R* method is an excellent way of studying such subjects that require more detailed types of knowledge. This format will also go far in helping you to compile the content you need to know. You may not grasp all the details, but you will be well on your way to improving your understanding of the material. At a later time, you can go back and memorize the sections that need to be learned by repetition.

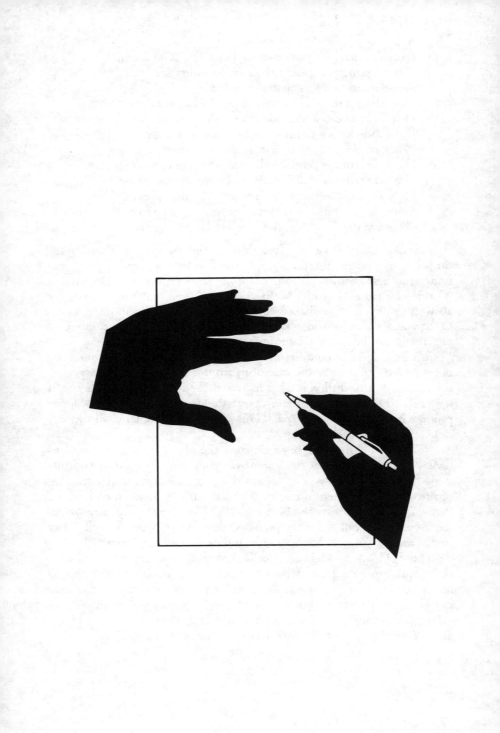

CHAPTER SIX

IMPROVING YOUR TEST TAKING

Taking a test is much like running a race. As the runner gets ready to run—following the rules of the race—so the student has to prepare for the test—obeying the instructions found on it. However, many a runner has lost a race because he has not paid close enough attention to the rules: when to start, how to pace himself, and where to finish. Even though the runner made careful preparation, he lost the race due to the oversight of a particular rule. Likewise, many a student has studied and reviewed all the material at hand, but he failed because he did not read the test instructions carefully.

Perhaps you are the kind of person that answers each question very slowly and thoughtfully, but forgets the time and ends up finishing only half the exam—a problem of pacing. Maybe you are the type of person that cannot recall important details on an objective test or the flow of thought for an essay exam—a problem of logical recall. Or, it could be that you do not approach a test with a plan of attack—a problem of strategy. This is not to mention the absent-minded student who comes to the examination without a pencil or pen. Or, he never thinks to take an extra writing instrument in case his fails—a problem of preparation. If any of these scenarios have been true for you, then this chapter will help. Hopefully the guidelines that follow will encourage you to overcome the fear of test taking, to properly prepare for the exam, as well as to tackle test taking with confidence.

1. ANXIETY ATTACK

Anxiety is a fact of life. We all get "butterflies" in our stomachs once in a while—even when we face an upcoming exam. Actually a little nervous energy can be a positive force that can help come test time. You do not want to become so lax that you lose that "cutting edge" that keeps you alert. Even the most outgoing people get queasy when they get up in front of an audience to speak or perform. Therefore, we need to deal with the fear of failing, the panic of not being able to recall a particular answer, or the terror of pulling a complete blank on a test.

As disciples of Christ, we should realize that the Bible exhorts us not to fear anyone (Matthew 10:28) or anything, but God alone

(Deuteronomy 6:2). This must be our attitude when we approach our fears—even the fear of taking a test. God knows our every weakness and how frail our earthly frames are (Hebrews 2:17-18). His Word and promises uphold us in time of need. Therefore, make it a matter of prayer—asking the Lord to help you overcome the fear of taking exams. Claim His promise in Isaiah 41:10, which says, "Fear thou not; for I am with thee: be not dismayed; for I am thy God: I will strengthen thee; yea, I will help thee; yea I will uphold thee with the right hand of my righteousness."

Once we have our fears under the authority of God's Word, then we can take a closer look at why some people fail—and how to overcome it. No doubt some do not care, or refuse to study; while others do not pay attention to the course requirements or misconstrue the instructions on the test itself. It may even be the "fear of success"—due to the fact that your parents or significant others will continually expect you to do well in the future. And what about those who cannot deal with competition—they always worry about the other guy?

Frankly, you will always encounter some kind of pressure in life—such as passing a driver's test to get your license, or meeting a deadline on your job. Instead of reinforcing the negative, try looking at this kind of pressure as *good*. A positive attitude can go a long way to helping you overcome your fears and succeed in life. Do not fall into the trap of always complaining about every test that comes along. Some people actually thrive on being miserable. It would be better to stop grumbling and start studying. Moreover, do not be swayed by these "complainers" either—they can be very convincing when it comes to getting your focus off of what is important and onto yourself. However, keep your thoughts on target, in regard to this whole process of learning; you will come to realize that this test is just another milestone in your educational experience. Also, do not bring all your personal problems into the exam with you, but go with a clear heart and mind. There is a time and place for everything, and this is the time to take the test!

Look at test taking as just a 45- or 60-minute period of time that will come and go quickly—faster than you might imagine. It is only a small slice of life, which will not make or break your career as a student. This is just another opportunity—yes, an opportunity—for you to perform under pressure. Simply do your level best, and move on. There are other things in life that will be waiting for you after you have finished your test. In the end, all those exams and quizzes that you take will give you a sense of success to some degree or another, so build on these triumphs and leave the rest to God.

2. PREPARING FOR AN EXAM

Test taking is a fact of life that each of us must learn to tackle with calmness and a positive attitude. Some of the exams we will face in our academic career are achievement tests, college entrance exams, and tests for entering graduate school. Even if you want to get your driver's license, you have to take a written test—and a road test. Test taking is here to stay. Therefore, you must learn how to properly prepare, since this is half the battle. Of course, you may be the kind of person who does well on test day; but hopefully you will find a few ideas here and there that will give you that extra "edge."

Much of what has been covered in the previous chapter "Improving Your Study Habits," especially under the subheadings "Taking Notes" and "Reading a New Textbook," will go a long way in guiding you in making the proper preparations for taking a test. There is no reason why you should cram for an exam. Even if you think cramming is the best method, it has been shown that your retention level drops off dramatically after twenty-four hours. In fact, after only five minutes of perusing new material, you will begin to lose what you have learned.

Therefore, your main goal should be to **review** what you have read and the notes you have taken. You also need to develop the proper "handles" for your memory to access the information you need. In this way, you can retain much more. Here is where such systems as the *SQ3R* method come in handy. As you study and read, build upon the basic outline of the material found in your text and hang all the new information on these cues. This should be done on a daily basis—overlapping your study time with the *review* of what you learned the previous day. Consequently, the flow of your understanding will continue unbroken.

Follow these simple steps:

1. Begin your daily study time by *reviewing* your notes from the previous day.
2. Study your course outline, which comes from the text's table of contents.
3. Examine the questions at the end of the section or chapter you are studying.
4. If there is required outside reading, track it down and begin reading at this time.
5. Take notes on the material—this will be the basis for your next day's *review*.

Therefore, the best way to prepare for that upcoming exam is to **study and review on a daily basis**—not in a last minute "cram session." Even though you may forget much of what you learned several days before, your note-taking and outlining skills will help you to mentally retrace and relearn the bulk of the material. Reinforcing the key points of each lesson on a daily basis will reduce your preparation time and help you easily remember the information for the test. An added feature to this plan is the time you will have to concentrate on your weak areas—those memory gliches that need extra work.

You may be tempted to go back and reread pages of your textbook to review for the exam. However, if you have properly outlined and highlighted the text, then you will not have much to reread—except the material that you marked off. If you have reviewed on a daily basis, then the vital information you need will stand out. However, the best way to study for an exam is to lay your text and notes aside and try to recall as much as possible. Form questions from the notes that *might* be on the test, and answer them from memory. Try to make up an acrostic or some other device to recall the main points. Diagrams, outlines, charts, and other creative means will help you to master those abstract concepts that seem to elude you.

Remember, your review sessions are to help you recall what you have learned in a *coherent* and *logical* manner. The person that waits to the last minute can never quite get a handle on what he is studying. He hopes beyond hope that all will fall together in an organized way at test time. Unfortunately, when an essay exam comes along, the person who crams for the test cannot put his thoughts down in either a logical or coherent fashion. In contrast, the wise student who is well-prepared and can get a good night's rest can take everything in stride. He can rise the next morning fresh and alert. Therefore, forget the all-nighters, and the "energy" drinks and cold showers to stay awake; and enjoy the peace of mind that comes from being properly prepared ahead of time.

The following system uses three-by-five cards. Each of the major points on the exam can be written on a separate index card for easy recall. Try this helpful technique the next time you prepare for a test.

How did world dictators start World War II?

CARD ONE

> *How did Communists take over Russia?*
>   1917—Communist revolution led by Lenin
>   1924—Stalin takes over; oppresses the people

CARD TWO

How did Mussolini work to destroy the peace?
   1922—Mussolini takes over Italy by force
   Lateran Treaty makes Pope head of Vatican City
   Mussolini becomes supreme ruler in Italy

CARD THREE

How did Hitler become a dictator in Germany?
   1930s—Depression hits Germany
   1933 —Hitler takes over

CARD FOUR

How did these dictators expand their empires?
   1931—Japan takes over Manchuria–part of China
   League of Nations is powerless to stop Japan

   1935—Mussolini enters Africa; Ethiopia taken
   1936—Franco fights Loyalist Communists–Spain
   1937—Japan invades China
   1938—Hitler invades Austria

CARD FIVE

How did World War II start?
   1939—Hitler attacks Poland from the west
   Britain & France declare war on Germany
   Russia attacks Poland—Poland is divided

Figure 6.1

3. Taking the Test

Obviously there are various kinds of tests: objective, essay, or oral exams. In addition, there are different types of objective tests: true-false, matching, fill-in-the-blank, and short answer. So you need to **develop a plan of attack** for each one. For example, the *essay test* requires you to understand and formulate the facts in a logical way. You cannot just write fast and furiously, divulging all the information that comes to mind. First, you must formulate your arguments in a coherent and logical manner. Likewise, the *oral exam* demands that you think on your feet, and the flow of reasoned thought must come from your memory—both the outline and the arguments. Whether it is an essay or oral exam, be aware of what you need to do: compare or contrast certain issues, defend a given point of view, or discuss a particular idea.

On the other hand, *objective exams* deal with facts and are designed to see if you can recall the information either found in your textbook or given in a lecture. Your particular opinions or ideas are not of interest to the one giving the test—only the content of the material is at stake. In the case of multiple choice or matching, you need to use the process of elimination or make an "educated" guess. If you do not know the answer at first sight, and you will not be penalized for guessing the wrong answer, then examine each alternative and determine which one best fits. Eliminate the obvious ones immediately, and then tackle those that are not so obvious.

If it is a historical question, try to see which answer coincides with the time period under consideration. If it is a content question, then choose the answer that meets all the clues found in the given information. If it is a cause-and-effect question, try to diagram it; or if it is a question of logic, then chart the flow of thought. In this way, you will be able to clarify the issues and sort out the answers. All of this boils down to four simple things to keep in mind:

1. Rely on your previous knowledge.
2. Exercise a little common sense.
3. Use the process of elimination.
4. Beware of "trick" questions.

Now comes the day you have been looking forward to—or you wish was behind you. Being on time for an exam, especially one like an SAT or other similar tests, will give you that peace of mind (if there is such a thing on test day) you need to get settled. Find out ahead of time where the exam is being given, and go there the day before so no mishap may arise on the way. Of course, if you are taking a test at home, all of the above does not apply—you will be completely relaxed, without a care in the world. When the time comes, you will be sitting poised on the edge of your chair, ready to begin. No doubt you have all the supplies you need: pens, pencils, a calculator (if allowed), and any other things required. Now you are ready to begin.

Here is a list of ideas that will help you make it through your exam with "flying colors":

- **Before you begin, pray.** Ask the Lord to help you recall what you have studied. If you have prepared, He can help you according to His will. But do not expect God to work in a vacuum.

- **Look over the test from beginning to end.** Notice how long it is and how it will be scored. Determine the value of each answer. And see if scratch paper or a calculator can be used.

- **Follow the test instructions explicitly.** Do not skim over them. You could miss an important guideline, which may cost you dearly. If the test is scannable, do not make any stray marks.

- **Determine how the exam is scored.** Normally the test is based on the number of correct answers; but occasionally wrong answers are penalized. Therefore, pace yourself accordingly.

- **Watch your time.** Give each section adequate time. Do not waste precious moments on difficult questions. Keep moving! If you are not penalized for wrong answers, try to finish all of them. If you are taking a timed test, pace yourself accordingly. Use your own watch because other clocks may not be reliable.

- **Check your work.** After you have finished the test, go back over your answers and check your spelling—especially if it is an essay exam. Reexamine any answers you marked as questionable.

- **For oral exams jot down key words**—nouns and verbs. These key terms will help you recall the whole idea. If you do not understand something, ask questions or have the information repeated.

- **Take any breaks that are offered.** Use the restroom, get a drink, or eat a candy bar. And if you get up-tight, stretch those tense muscles to start refreshed. However, do not waste time.

- **Take some time off and relax** after you have completed a major test. Since you have been flexing those "mental muscles" for the last several days, you need to take a break. Ease up and recreate.

4. MEMORIZING THE MATERIAL

When it comes to taking a test or reciting something in a classroom setting, it is your ability to memorize that needs to be sharpened. However, this power to recall what you have learned is a skill that few seek to acquire. But we all admire those who can recite a passage from God's Word, a poem that is meaningful, or a speech that has been prepared, without any qualms. Such a person needs to remember key ideas, exact wording, and the precise gestures to deliver the speech properly. Like an actor who masters the work of a playwright, so the orator needs to learn the skill of memorization.

Most of us know of the "blood, sweat, and tears" method of rote memorization. Since we all need to recall facts and dates from history, formulas from science and mathematics, literary characters and plots, and entire poems or speeches, we usually turn to the tried and true approach of repetition. However, a practical way to build our memory skills without the pain is to learn to "code" the data we must know. Coding is a computer term that refers to making a file *stand out* in some way from other information that you have compiled, so it can be retrieved easily. Likewise, you will be able to access needed data from your "memory banks" come test time or when you have to give something orally. The question is: "How do I learn to *code* the information I need to know?"

The whole idea behind the "coding" of data in our memory is to *visually associate* the bit of information that needs to be remembered with some *nonsensical image*. You conjure up some ridiculous notion in your mind that can be identified with whatever you want to recall. For instance, let us say that you have to remember that William Shakespeare was born in *1564*. How could you recall this date for your next exam? You could think of the year 1964 minus 400, which equals the year this famous playwright was born. The year 1964 is closer in time to the present, and the last digit (4) multiplied by 100 gives you the number of years you need to subtract from 1964 to get the exact year of his birth. Picture Shakespeare in bell-bottom trousers and a flower in his hair—the typical '60s look!

Perhaps you have a series of items that you need to recall on an examination that is coming up in the near future. How can you successfully remember all this information accurately and logically? Let us say, by way of example, you need to know all the names and descriptions of the bones or group of bones from the tips of your fingers to your collar bone. Examine the following table, including a list of zany memory devices:

	Name	Description	Memory Device
1.	**phalanges**	fingers	*fallen geese*
2.	**metacarpals**	palm	*metal car / pals*
3.	**carpus**	wrist	*carp / us*
4.	**ulna**	inside bone of forearm	*Alma*
5.	**radius**	outside bone of forearm	*raid / us*
6.	**olecranon**	elbow	*old cra'on*
7.	**humerus**	upper arm	*humor / us*
8.	**clavicle**	collar bone	*clay vehicle*

Figure 6.2

If you had to memorize all 206 of the bones in our bodies, it would be a challenge; but these eight will do for now. The best way to tackle this assignment is to tie all these parts together in an amusing sentence, which can easily be "retrieved": The *fallen geese* were found in a *metal car*. These *pals* joined the *carp* to attack *us*. *Alma* drove as the rest planned to *raid us*, with an *ole cra'on* for a weapon. This did *humor us*, but we escaped in our *clay vehicle*. This funny story may not capture your imagination, but you can make up your own. The sky is the limit, so try your expert hand at trying to humor us—no pun intended. Perhaps you could even set it to music.

There are other ways you can create *visual associations* that will improve your capacity to memorize important facts. The following acronym, "**a beard**," may help:

ALLITERATE	The repetition of the first sound, usually consisting of a consonant or a group of letters in two or more words of a phrase, poetry, etc.
BIZZARE	If at all possible, make these visual associations as bizzare or unusual as you can—the zanier, the better.
EMOTIVE	Create some kind of emotion when using these associations. You want to evoke joy, sadness, pain, or disgust.

ACRONYMS	An acronym is a word made up of the first letter(s) in a list of words (e.g., *radar—ra*dio *d*etecting *a*nd *r*anging).
RHYMES	Perhaps you recall a jingle you heard on the radio or television—which sticks. If so, then rhymes might help you to memorize.
DRAMATIZE	Create some kind of action-packed adventure that pulses with energy—like geese and fish attacking with an *ole cra'on*, and the victims on the run!

At first glance, this may seem like a considerable amount of work—formulating such zany imaginations. However, as you hone this crazed-filled exercise, it will become second nature to you. In fact, this touches the tip of the old proverbial "iceberg." There are many other memory devices that can be employed, such as mnemonics, acrostics, abbreviations, linking two facts together at the same time, turning abstract ideas into concrete objects, pegging and linking, and the list goes on. Be sure to read the appendix by Gary DeMar called "Memory Mechanics," which highlights these and more. The memory is truly a gift from God that each of us should treasure and nurture—filling it with all that is pleasing to Him.

Chapter Seven

Improving Your Life by Reading

Finally, brethren, whatsoever things are true, whatsoever things are honest, whatsoever things are just, whatsoever things are pure, whatsoever things are lovely, whatsoever things are of good report; if there be any virtue, and if there be any praise, think on these things.
Philippians 4:8

Reading is one of the few pleasures of life that *no* one can afford *not* to engage in. Yet this affordable pleasure has fallen on hard times, much to the horror of those who truly love reading and know the powerful wonders that this enjoyable pastime can bestow. However, if you have never experienced the exhilaration of perusing a good story—or if your heart and mind have never surged with sheer joy, anxious fear, or absolute rage—you have undoubtedly neglected a world of the utmost delight. Through the magical wonder of books you can visit enchanted, faraway places that may startle or astound the innermost resources of your mind. Free access to this wonderful world of books can broaden the scope of your horizons, introducing you to realms previously beyond your reach. This world of marvels is as close as the sensation of your fingertips—and the gaze of your eyes.

Over and above the mere pleasure that the written word may provide, and of far more significance to your success in school, is the value of your reading as a student. The one who has learned to read has overcome the greatest challenge a student can face in studying. In addition, this person will have gained the skill of concentration—by being held in suspense for hours by the pages of an exciting novel or by braving the intrigue of a provocative book. Such a student will build and expand his vocabulary as well, thus overcoming one of the first obstacles he will face in studying a textbook. Therefore, you can insure your future—whatever that may be—by reading, both for the sake of your studies and for pleasure.

As you read, you will become aware of the various styles that sentences may take—simple and complex. Descriptive passages will come alive, and technical data will be understood more readily. Thus, the information that you incorporate into your thought processes through reading will help you in your study of history, literature, and science. And these areas of study in turn will enrich your understanding because they have been used as the backdrop for all well-written stories, articles, and novels. All that you have gained through what you have read will give you an advantage in your future studies—enhancing your appreciation and comprehension of all that is to come.

Here are a few guidelines that will help you succeed in your reading:

1. **Choose a book that you want to read for pleasure.** Make sure it is one that you can finish quickly. Summertime is best for this kind of leisurely reading. Set a goal of perusing one or two good books per week. Then during the school year read at least one per month.

2. **Look for books that are considered *classics*.** These all-time favorites have been tested over the years and have not lost their appeal. These are very helpful for those who desire to build a good foundation for further study—at home or at schools of higher learning.

3. **Aim to read fifteen minutes a day.** You do not have to limit yourself to this, but plan to if other priorities demand it. You will be amazed at how many books you will be able to complete in such a small amount of time.

4. **Do not forget to keep your trusty dictionary close by.** It only takes but a moment to look up a new word and discover its meaning. Just imagine all the terms you will be able to add to your inventory of words—enriching your future writing and speaking.

5. **Maintain good reading habits.** Finding that quiet nook, where you can get away from it all, will pay dividends. The television, CD player, or stereo can break your concentration at those critical moments that deserve your utmost attention. And only use good lighting.

6. **Encourage others to read what you have read.** Recommending a good book, or telling others about an insightful article, will enhance your friendships and reinforce what you have learned. Discuss your views and argue the strengths or weaknesses of your readings.

7. **Read with a worldview in mind.** The underlying principles of an author affect what he writes, and ultimately what you read. So know what you believe. You will be held accountable for what you read. "Finally, brethren, whatsoever things are true, ... honest, ... just, ... pure, ... lovely, ... of good report; if there be any virtue, and if there be any praise, think on these things" (Philippians 4:8).

APPENDIX I

MEMORY MECHANICS

by Gary DeMar

"I forgot!"

You have said it thousands of times with embarrassment, vexation, and self-reproach. In attempting to remember speeches, price lists, studies, statistics, names, and faces you have depended on the old, tiresome method of repetition to stamp them on your memory—and it went back on you at the critical moment.

This is all unnecessary. You have the proper mental equipment, but neglect and wrong methods have caused it to deteriorate.

Your memory is actually the most wonderful instrument in the world. You need only to know how to use it to do things that appear marvelous. The purpose of these lessons is to afford you a real opportunity for improvement.

David M. Roth

Our brain is a magnificent creation. A typical adult's brain contains fifteen billion to one hundred billion neurons. If we accept the lower estimate, this means that you and I can remember two-to-the-ten-billionth-power bits of information. How big is this number? Well, it would take you ninety years to write it out if you wrote a zero per second. If we take the larger number of neurons, this would be equivalent to ten billion encyclopedia pages of information. The brain is a very big place in a very small space.

Some see the brain as a highly evolved machine. It's not. There is something unique about the human brain and its relationship with the mind. While a computer searches all the possibilities before it can come up with a correct answer, the brain evaluates, sorts, compares, discards, and formulates. There is an evaluation process going on that no computer can match.

The key word here is *evaluating*. By placing a value on a bit of information, we let it advance to the forefront or recede to form a part of a larger picture. We can do this temporarily or permanently, and we can convert the images later if we want to. No tape recorder, camera, or even a computer can do all of this. Computers, in fact, are just very fast, efficient morons, with neither imagination nor common sense. It takes a computer four minutes to work out the right combination for a Rubik's Cube, considering every possible turn until all the correct ones have been made. An efficient teenager can do it in two minutes, and the sixteen-year-old 1982 World Champion did it in 22.95 seconds!

Joan Minninger

But as scientists learn more about memory, they are beginning to realize that there is no single entity called "memory." Consider an amnesiac. Clive Wearing once was an expert on Renaissance music and a producer for the British Broadcasting Corporation (BBC). Not long ago he came down with a rare form of encephalitis, an inflammation of the brain, which left him with a memory span of only a few seconds. He cannot recall a single event in the past. He couldn't tell you what he just had for lunch, even if he had eaten the meal ten minutes before. But not all his memory patterns have been wiped out. He can sing and conduct a choir. His musical ability is still intact. Wearing's wife, Deborah, says, he "is trapped forever in the groove of a scratched record." Memory, then, is multifaceted and much more difficult to describe and define than was once thought. "It seems, then, that some sections of the mind's archives store facts (names, images, events), while others store procedures (recollections of how to do things)."

While it's important to understand what memory is, it's more important for a student to understand how it works and how to improve it. Students want a more efficient memory so that studying will be easier. This chapter will introduce you to methods that will expand your ability to remember.

TWELVE MEMORY TECHNIQUES

The ability to have a good memory is present with each of us. And while superior intelligence might be an asset in developing a good memory, it's not a prerequisite. Memory is more a technique than a gift.

Memory is the ability to attach unknown ideas or facts to known ideas or facts. Parents transfer basic sounds to an infant, and the infant mimics the parents. This continues with words, phrases, and sentences. Learning the alphabet leads to learning words, words are worked into sentences, and sentences are turned into complete and workable ideas. Not much thought is given to all this. It just seems so "natural." But listen to any two-year-old struggle with simple words and phrases. In time, he learns to put all those new sounds into coherent thoughts. What began as babbling turns into beautiful speech. One word turns into thousands.

There are times when a single event that happens in a split second is recorded in your mind for a lifetime. It can be recalled at any time with no trouble. On November 22, 1963, President John F. Kennedy was assassinated in Dallas, Texas. I can remember where I was and what I was doing. But there is little else I remember of that day. In fact, there's not much in that year that I remember. You probably have similar memory patterns. What makes these events "stick," while others seem to be as slippery as teflon? The key to a good memory is association: linking something you know with something you want to know.

1. MNEMONICS

Your ability to memorize can improve by using devices and methods called *mnemonics* [pronounced nee-MON-iks or na-MON-iks]. The word comes from the same Greek root as that of *Mnemosyne*, the goddess of memory who was the mother of the nine sister muses who presided over the arts and sciences. (Did she have difficulty remembering all their names?) Our English word *mnemonic* means "helpful to memory."

Basically, all you must do is force yourself in unnatural and infrequent areas of learning to do what has been natural for years. Most learning comes by way of *associations*. You connect, associate, what you do know with what you do not know. You look for some relationship between the *new material* and the *familiar material*. While there may not be a subject connection (e.g., room and house), there may be an auditory connection ("In fourteen hundred and ninety-*two* Columbus sailed the ocean *blue*"). *Two* and *blue* have no subject connection, but they do sound alike. This is a forced memory connection.

If I were to ask you to name the Great Lakes, you might be able to remember two or three of them. But if I associate the five Great Lakes with something you already know, like HOMES, you will never forget them again: *H*uron, *O*ntario, *M*ichigan, *E*rie, and *S*uperior.

Many young children learned the word "arithmetic" as their first big word this way: *A* rat in Tom's house may eat Tom's ice cream.

The colors of the light spectrum, *r*ed, *o*range, *y*ellow, *g*reen, *b*lue, *i*ndigo, *v*iolet, can make up a fictitious man's name, Roy G. Biv.

The cranial nerves always present a problem for first-year medical students. The following memory device is a standard to remember *o*lfactory, *o*ptic, *o*culomotor, *t*rochlear, *t*rigeminal, *a*bducens, *f*acial, *a*uditory, *g*lossopharyngeal, *v*agus, *s*pinal accessory, and *h*ypoglossal: "*O*n *O*ld *O*lympus' *T*owering *T*op, *A* *F*riar *A*nd *G*reek *V*iewed *S*ome *H*ops."

The tribes of Israel: *J*udah, *I*ssachar, *M*anasseh, *B*enjamin, *R*euben, *A*sher, *N*aphtali, *D*an, *S*imeon, *E*phraim, *G*ad, and *Z*ebulun. If the tribal names are unfamiliar, look for a way of associating the *unfamiliar* tribal names with something *familiar*. You might try making up a little song, visualizing them on a map of Israel, or memorizing them in groups of three or four. (This is why your phone number and Social Security number have dashes between groups of numbers. It's much easier to remember a long number if it is broken down in smaller groups.)

Suppose that instead of following one of these devices (all good ones), you try taking the first letters of each tribal name to see if you can make something familiar with them. First you try B-R-I-M-S A-N-D J-E-G-Z. While it might be helpful, in time you would have difficulty remembering it because it isn't familiar enough. You try again and come up with J-I-M B-R-A-N-D-S E-G-Z. A name is easy to remember, and you can visualize twelve eggs with farmer Jim Brand picking them up. The only variation you have to make is to change the plural for eggs (the *z* sound) to EGZ (*z* substituting for the plural of egg).

It's easy to move from the tribes of Israel to the sons of Israel (Jacob). Two of the sons of Israel are not listed among the tribal allotments by name: Joseph and Levi. But we still have twelve tribes. Ephraim and Manasseh, we learn, are not the sons of Israel, but his grandsons. They are Joseph's sons, the same Joseph who is not listed among the twelve tribes. Levi is given cities throughout the tribal allotments. Ephraim and Manasseh are added to the other ten tribes and make up Joseph's inheritance.

2. ACRONYMS

An **acronym** is a word made up of the first letters of a list of names, items, places, etc. HOMES is a good example. You're probably familiar with FACE, an acronym used to help children remember the notes between the lines on the treble clef. In order to make an acronym work, you may have to reorder the list several times. While VIBGYOR might do for the light spectrum—it sounds more like some extraterrestrial being thrashing about with a laser weapon that emits the light spectrum—Roy G. Biv is probably better. If an acronym just doesn't work, you'll need to go on to some other technique.

3. Acrostics

An *acrostic* is very similar to an acronym. In an acronym the initials are pronounced to form a new word, either real or something pronounceable (e.g., NATO, NASA, HUD, etc.). An acrostic uses initials that are not pronounced but are used to form new words that make a sentence. For example, *Every Good Boy Does Fine* teaches a beginning music student the notes of the treble clef that appear on the lines: E-G-B-D-F. A student of biology devised the following: *Kings Play Cards On Fairly Good Soft Velvet*, for kingdom, phylum, class, order, family, genus, species, variety. You can remember the planets with this mnemonic device: *My Very Excellent Mother Just Sells Nuts Until Passover*, for Mercury, Venus, Earth, Mars, Jupiter, Saturn, Neptune, Uranus, and Pluto.

4. Visualization

"A picture is worth a thousand words." If that's true, then the mind can save you a lot of words. You can picture almost anything. Picture what you read. Turn abstractions into visual ideas that have a close association, either in content or sound.

> *Eye-pictures are the most accurate of mental impressions.* And because the mind has this wonderful ability to see pictures long after the disappearance of the original pictures that the real eye made on the mind, we speak of the *mind's eye*, and of seeing in our *mind's eye*. The scientific name for the *mind's eye* is visualization, and the ability to use this wonderful faculty is invaluable to you."
>
> *David M. Roth*

In time, the more you use the material, the artificial visual association will fade. Your mind will move directly to the idea. Visualize the three branches of government as a triangle with each side representing one branch. Then visualize that triangle perched on a *branch* of a cherry tree in Washington, D.C. Sure, it's not always this easy. But this method will take you pretty far.

One adaptation of the visualization technique is the "Location System." Roman orators commonly used the *loci* system to remember the components of a speech. They didn't have the advantage of a teleprompter or note cards. In this system, major parts of the speech were associated with a certain route from the speaker's home to the Forum where he was to give his address. Along the way, he would associate a familiar landmark with the points of his address—one landmark with one point in the speech. As he delivered his speech, he would recall the landmarks in order of their place along the route and each speech component would be recalled as well. The following story is told of a Russian's ability to recall items that were memorized years before.

> A Russian renowned for his memory could hear a list of fifty words and recite them back without error fifteen years later. As he heard each item he mentally placed it along Moscow's Gorky Street, outside a shop he knew well. To remember the items, he took a mental walk down Gorky and picked them up one at a time.
>
> "Memory," Newsweek (9/29/86)

If you have a group of similar concepts to learn, try to place them in a house with various rooms. For example, if you have to learn the names of the [Presidents] from the [eighteenth]-century to the present, you can choose one room for each century. Then place the [Presidents] for a particular century in different locations in a room (e.g., the living room), sitting on chairs, sitting at the piano, standing by the window, sitting on the sofa, etc. By visualizing the room and the furniture, you can easily recall the names by their location. Your own home or familiar building would be the best *loci* to choose. You could associate each [President's] name with an article of furniture that can easily be recalled for the test.

5. VOCALIZATION, RHYMES, AND JINGLES

Some people are better auditory learners. Reading something aloud and emphasizing the main points with greater inflection may help. Most of us learned the alphabet this way. One way to remember names, for example, is to repeat the name of the individual you were just introduced to. Hearing it again helps the memory process.

Most of us can remember commercials because they have catchy tunes or clever associations: "The Coke® Side of Life"; or for Pringles® potato chips, "Once you pop, you can't stop." How did you learn when to set your clocks ahead and back every year? "Spring ahead, fall back." In April (spring) we move our clocks ahead one hour (*spring* forward). In October (fall) we turn our clocks back one hour (*fall* backward).

6. ABBREVIATION

Sometimes it helps if you abbreviate a long section of material into its essential parts. For example:

THE TEN COMMANDMENTS

1. No other gods	6. No murder
2. No graven images	7. No adultery
3. Name of Lord	8. No stealing
4. Sabbath rest	9. No false witness
5. Honor mom and dad	10. No coveting

Instead of ten commandments to learn, you now have two groups of five commandments. You can shorten this even further by leaving off the negatives, for abbreviation purposes only. Be forewarned, however, there was a Bible published that left the "not" out of the seventh commandment. It was called the "Adulterer's Bible."

Our nation's Constitution had attached to it ten brief amendments. Here's a handy way to learn the basics of each one:

THE "BILL OF RIGHTS"

(The first Ten Amendments to the Constitution)

1. Freedom of religion, speech, press, assembly, and petition
2. Right to bear arms
3. Quartering of soldiers
4. Search and seizure
5. Personal legal protection
   a. Indictment
   b. Double jeopardy
   c. Self-incrimination
   d. Legal trial
   e. Private property
6. Speedy, public trial
7. Common law suits
8. Bail, fines, sentence
9. Protection of rights not aforementioned
10. State's rights

You can add your visualization techniques to many of these. Freedom of religion could be represented by a cross or Bible, speech by a podium or megaphone, press by a newspaper or book, assembly by a crowd or a group of picketers holding signs, and petition by a scroll with names written on it. Arms could be represented by a rifle or a revolver. Quartering soldiers could be remembered by visualizing troops coming to a home and hoping to gain entrance by paying a quarter. You can finish the visualization with your own associations.

7. MEMORY CONNECTIONS

How can you remember a sequence of events? All those bits of meandering memory mechanics might make me mad miming mindless muddle. Good point. How can you best remember a list of events that have to be in order?: two facts at a time. By associating the first fact with the second fact, the second fact with the third fact, the third fact with the fourth fact, etc., you can learn a whole string of events, two facts at a time. Here's how the "Link Method" works:

THE MINOR PROPHETS

1. **Hosea** = *Hose* spraying out *jewels* instead of water.
2. **Joel** = *Jewels* falling on *a moss-covered* arrow.
3. **Amos** = *A moss-covered* arrow aimed at an *oboe* player.
4. **Obadiah** = *The oboe* player meets *Jonah* in a whale.
5. **Jonah** = *Jonah* goes to a *microphone* to sing.
6. **Micah** = The microphone sends out a *hum*.
7. **Nahum** = *The hum* makes the *haberdasher's* hat vibrate.
8. **Habakkuk** = *The haberdasher's* hat is blown off by a *zephyr*.
9. **Zephaniah** = *The zephyr* blows it to an old *hag*.
10. **Haggai** = *The hag* scares old *Zack*.
11. **Zechariah** = *Zack* runs to *Malachi the mailman* for help.
12. **Malachi**= *Malachi the mailman* delivers a closed Bible.

Associate each unfamiliar minor prophet with a visual sound-alike word. Visualize a *hose* (Hosea) spewing out *jewels* (Joel). The *jewels* come out and smash into a man aiming *a moss* (Amos)-covered arrow at a man playing an *oboe* (Obadiah). His playing is so bad that he is swallowed by a whale where he happens to meet *Jonah*. Jonah tells his story using a *mi*crophone (Micah), but the only sound that anyone hears is a gentle *hum* (Nahum), etc.

Once you recall the hose, the visualization process takes over. The memory sequence starts with only two minor prophets in view at any one time. Once the memory link is made, the first minor prophet fades away and the new association takes over. This technique can be used with any sequence of events.

8. FROM THE ABSTRACT TO THE CONCRETE

Abstract ideas are some of the most difficult concepts to remember. There are few memory "handles" for your mind to hold on to. An abstract idea has to be turned into something concrete. For example, how can you make existentialism concrete? For a philosophy test you have to remember that Heidegger, Sartre, and Kierkegaard are existentialists. You know that existentialists believe that "existence precedes essence." Exist sounds like "exit." When you come into the world (a type of existence) you "exit" your mother's body. And guess who's greeting you when you enter the world? *Heidi*, Captain James T. *Kirk* of the Starship Enterprise, and *Ser*geant (pronounced *sar*jent) York, the decorated World War I army hero. You can visualize a delivery room at a hospital with Heidi dressed up in her mountain-climbing clothes, Captain Kirk in his ship's captain attire, and Alvin York in his sergeant's uniform.

Here's a list of some abstract concepts and a list of concrete equivalents:

ABSTRACT CONCEPT	CONCRETE SYMBOL
1. Intelligence or mind	1. Brain
2. Grief	2. Someone in tears
3. Peace	3. Dove or olive branch
4. Ignorance	4. Dunce cap
5. Security	5. Padlock or vault
6. Hope	6. Anchor
7. Speed	7. Sprinter or race car
8. Language	8. Dictionary
9. Happiness	9. Mask with a smile
10. Death	10. Coffin

9. PEGGING AND LINKING

Have you ever had trouble remembering numbers, dates, or a long list of related facts or dates? Well, do I have a system for you. Numbers and dates are abstract by themselves. You can have twelve eggs to make a dozen, twelve inches to make a foot, twelve tribes to make up the nation Israel, and twelve apostles to make up the number of men Jesus chose to be His closest disciples. It's difficult to make a number stand out as something more than a number. What if you have to remember various dates for the many battles that occurred during World War II? Did it happen on May 12, 1943 or May 13, 1945? Consider sixty events strung out over a period of five years. But what if each date could be turned into a picture? The month of May could be represented by a flower ("April Showers bring May *Flowers*"), twenty-three becomes gnome, and 1945 becomes tub and rail. A battle on this day would be associated with a flower shading a sleeping gnome who has just finished collecting a tub full of rails. How did I come up with this? Let me show you.

The pegging system is a comprehensive memory device that uses a number system that corresponds to the letters of the alphabet and their *sounds*. Keep in mind that the *sounds* are what's important, not the letter. For example,

- **t** and **d** represent the number 1 (one down stroke of letters, and both sound alike)
- **n** represents the number 2 (2 down strokes of letter)
- **m** represents the number 3 (3 down strokes of letter)
- **r** represents the number 4 (fou*r*)
- **l** represents the number 5 (L is the Roman numeral for 50)
- **j**, soft **g**, **ch**, and **sh** represent the number 6 (**j** [a backward 6], **g** [an upside down 6], **ch** and **sh** all sound alike)
- **k** and hard **g** represent the number 7 (**k** has a backward leaning 7)
- **f** and **v** represent the number 8 (a script **f** makes an 8)
- **p** and **b** represent the number 9 (**p** is a backward 9, **b** is a backward and upside down 9)
- **s**, soft **c**, and **z** represent 0

Other letters that *sound like* the above letters represent the same numerical value. For example, a word with a hard **c** and hard **g** sound would be a 7 along with k. A soft **c** sound (when it sounds like an s) would be a 0 as in daises, which would mean 100. A **v** could substitute for an **f** (have or half), a **p** for a **b** (pat or bat). This really is not very complicated, but it does take a little time to learn.

The following letters have *no numerical value* (all vowels and the letters that make up the word why):

A E I O U and *W H Y*

I'll take you through the first ten words/numbers to show you how it works.

1. **hat** (**h** and **a** have no numerical value, **t** is 1)
2. **hen** (**h** and **e** have no numerical value, **n** is 2)
3. **ham** (**h** and **a** have no numerical value, **m** is 3)
4. **hare** (**h**, **a**, & **e** have no numerical value, **r** is 4)
5. **hill** (**h** and **i** have no numerical value, the sound **l** is 5)
6. **jaw** (**j** is a backward 6, **a** and **w** have no numerical value)
7. **cow** (**c** is a hard **k** sound, **o** and **w** have no numerical value)
8. **hive** (**h**, **i**, and **e** have no numerical value, **v** sounds like **f** which in script looks like an 8)
9. **ape** (**a** and **e** have no value, **p** is a backward 9)
10. **toes** (**t** is 1, **o** and **e** have no numerical value, the *sound* of **z** in the **s** is 0)

You associate the first word, hat, with the second word hen. Then associate hen with ham. You want to make up some wild associations so you will never forget them. Continue until you learn all ten this way (there are one hundred words to learn). Once you have the ten associated, you can put ten unfamiliar words with the ten now familiar words—by associating **hat** with the first new word, **hen** with the second, **ham** with the third, and so forth. Since you know the ten linking words, it's just a matter of recalling one word at a time until you get all ten. Theoretically, you could learn a list of one hundred items in order in less than thirty minutes and recall it the next day for a test.

What about the numbers? Notice that h-a-t has an **h** and an **a**, two letters that have no numerical value. The **t** represents 1. So it is with all the words. Numbers can be translated into words, and words can be *visualized* and *associated*. So, an abstract number like **1903** (the year of the first flight by the Wright Brothers) becomes two words: **tub** (t is 1, **u** has no numerical value, and **b** is 9) and **ham** (h has no numerical value, **a** has no numerical value, and **m** is 3). From this you get the Wright Brothers delivering a new *tub* filled with a huge smoked *ham* to celebrate their first flight.

There's much more to this system. Even if you never use it, it's a lot of fun. Here are a few books that go into great detail with all the specifics and applications:

1. David M. Roth, *The Famous Roth Memory Course* (New York: Sun Dial Press, Inc., 1918, 1934). This book is no longer in print. You may be able to find it in a used bookstore. It is very rare. All the modern memory books use Roth's system, but few give him the credit he deserves.

2. Harry Lorayne and Jerry Lucas, *The Memory Book* (New York: Ballantine Books, 1974). This book was a number one coast-to-coast bestseller. In their chapter on "Some History of the Art," they state that it is their "pleasure to bring the art of trained memory back into the foreground." Unfortunately, not once do they mention David M. Roth. You can find this book in most used bookstores. It may still be in print.

3 James D. Weinland, *How to Improve Your Memory* (New York: Barnes & Noble, 1957). This is a very helpful book. He mentions Roth (p. 108).

10. The Six Serving Men

One of the best ways to remember is to ask questions. When you want to get the basic information out of a lesson, follow the prescription of Rudyard Kipling:

> I keep six honest serving men
> (They taught me all I knew);
> Their names are *What* and *Why* and *When*
> and *How* and *Where* and *Who*.

These indicators will help you retrieve key information. Since you now know the serving men, recalling the needed information comes more easily. Also, it's a great way of organizing information that you read. Put the six serving men across a sheet of paper and fill in the questions as you read.

11. Flash Cards

In order to work for the Post Office, you must take zip code tests on a frequent basis. Sometimes mail comes in without a zip code. You do not have time to look up the street number and name. You must know it *immediately.* Time is money. There are thousands of streets in our large cities. You are required to know the zip code of nearly every street in the city if you work as a letter sorter. The only way to do it is with flash cards. The name of the street on one side, the zip code on the other.

This technique can be used for learning vocabulary words for foreign language study. All the memory techniques discussed thus far can be applied to the flash card approach. Be sure to mix the order periodically so you will not memorize them based on familiarity with the previous card.

12. *Preview* plus SQ3R

For broad review learning you will not be able to use mnemonic devices. Another method is needed. Mnemonic devices, however, will come in handy within the broad concepts. In 1946 Dr. Francis P. Robinson wrote *Effective Study*, in which he explained a study method that contained five simple steps: *S*urvey, *Q*uestion, *R*ead, *R*ecite, *R*eview: SQ3R. I've added another: *P*review.

The following is a brief explanation of this very popular and effective system.

PREVIEW
Look at any introductory material that is supplied with the material that you are about to survey. Is there an introduction, preface, or foreword? Check out the table of contents.

SURVEY
Reading boldfaced type, topic sentences, summary paragraphs, and review questions will give you an idea of the contents of the assignment.

QUESTION
After you have completed the survey, ask yourself what will be the important information contained in the assignment. Questioning will also help you to link the information in the assignment to what you already know. An easy way to create the questions is to turn the boldfaced type or the topic sentences into questions. Some texts supply questions at the end of each chapter.

READ
Read for ideas—especially to answer the questions you have created or read. Read one section at a time, and then go to the next step.

RECITE
Answer the questions you have asked, without looking at your notes or at the notebook. After you have finished answering the questions, go on to the next section of the assignment. Read it, and answer the questions you have asked. Continue reading and reciting until you have finished the assignment.

REVIEW
After you have finished the assignment, look away from the book, go over your notes, and get a comprehensive grasp of the complete assignment.

The *SQ3R* formula will go a long way in helping you formulate the context of what you need to know. You may not pick up some of the *particulars*, but you can always go back and spend specialized time on the rote memorization sections.

Pulling It All Together

All of the above techniques can be used to memorize large sections of poetry and prose. Why not try your hand at Abraham Lincoln's *Gettysburg Address*. But before you make the attempt, consider these suggestions.

First, understand the setting for the *Gettysburg Address*. Why did President Lincoln give it? Where did he give it? What are the circumstances surrounding the event? This will help you understand the terms being used and give you a feel for the time: civil war, battlefield, final resting place, brave men living and dead, etc. The more familiar you are with something, the easier it will be for you to memorize it.

Second, familiarize yourself with the entire address before you begin to memorize it. Understand the flow of thought. Anticipate what will come next.

Third, divide up the address into smaller sections. Find its natural rhythm: "Fourscore and seven years ago / our fathers brought forth on this continent / a new nation / conceived in liberty / and dedicated to the proposition that all men are created equal."

Fourth, apply some of the memory techniques, especially visualization and linking. You might even want to try locating the address on a battlefield while you walk through it, associating portions of the address with items you might find there. Creating a sing-song effect might be of some help. Combining these techniques could also prove helpful.

Fifth, when all else fails, repetition or vocal emphasis can get you over a sticking point....

CONCLUSION

Memory, like all mental activity, takes practice. When we were very young, memorizing was easy; it was natural. As we grew older, the memorizing process was dulled because we no longer learned at the rate we did when we were infants. What we had to learn became less and less, and the process we used to remember changed. Our initial experience with memory was not in the classroom or over books. Memory work seemed so natural that it wasn't work at all.

Times have changed and so has our ability to memorize. But maybe we can capture some of that youthful technique. The process has not really changed. In fact, we still use it; we're just not aware of it. This chapter has given you some tools to help you revitalize your memory processes.

We are all impressed with people who sport a prodigious memory. There are even an infrequent number of savants who can remember seemingly endless lists of names and numbers. Who will ever forget

Dustin Hoffman's portrayal of Raymond in the Academy-Award winning *Rainman* and the restaurant scene with the telephone book and toothpicks? Given enough time, he would have memorized the entire telephone book.

Then there is Leslie Lemke who after hearing a song played just once can duplicate it on a piano without missing a note. Leslie has never had a piano lesson. In fact, he is blind and severely retarded. His memory is extraordinary only in this one area. Beyond this unique ability, however, Leslie is completely dependent on the care of loving family members. This single gift of musical memory has not equipped him to live beyond the confines of his sheltered existence.

Call out any date, and there are a rare number of people who can tell you the day of the week on which the date falls. No calculator is needed. No pencil or paper is required. In a matter of seconds the answer is given.

> While no single theory put forth thus far can explain all savants, there is one single trait that all savants do have in common. That trait is superior memory. Leslie Lemke has a seemingly endless repertoire of pieces that he has heard only once but can recall perfectly years later. Richard Wawro visits a marketplace in Poland and several years later paints from memory a picture of it—in exquisite and minute detail. Ellen listens to an entire opera once or twice and then sings it back without error. George remembers what the weather was on every day of his adult life.
>
> *Darold A. Treffert*

This is the world of the savant. An extraordinary memory is all they seem to have. While we might envy them in this single area, none of us would trade places with any of them.

Memory for memory's sake is not much good to anyone, except maybe the few who make a living by demonstrating their ability to memorize almost anything. Memory, if it is going to be helpful, has to be put to some good use. While most of us do not have the ability of a savant in the area of memory demonstration, our gifts more than overshadow their extraordinary talent. God has equipped all of us with the ability to memorize. Practice will make it work better.

APPENDIX II

RESOURCE MATERIALS

If you are seeking a more in-depth approach to the improving of your study skills, then one of the following books or series of books will be of interest to you. Not all of these are from a Christian perspective, so beware! But a short synopsis after each entry will guide you in your continued search for a thorough plan of study. For more listings, check your local library under "how to study" in the card catalog. You could also ask your parents, pastor, or trusted Christian friend for additional insights and resources on studying from a Christian perspective.

Surviving College Successfully: A Complete Manual for the Rigors of Academic Combat (Brentwood, TN: Wolgemuth & Hyatt, publishers, Inc., 1988), by Gary DeMar, is an excellent book for someone planning to pursue a higher level of education. This approach has two main goals: to prepare the student for the spiritual warfare that he will face on any university campus—Christian or not; and to develop good study skills for inside and outside the classroom. The first half of the book is  helpful in understanding various worldviews and satanic schemes that you will confront even if you do not plan to go to college. The second half may be what you are looking for in advanced approaches to studying. (This title is out of print but can be found on used-book websites or at your local library.)

Ron Fry's **How To Study Program,** *6th Edition* (Clifton Park, NY: Delmar Cengage Learning, 2006), is a delightful series of paperbacks suited to the student who wants to approach studying with a sense of humor. Although these seven books are not written from a Christian point of view, they are helpful in breaking down each area of studying into bite-size pieces. Each book covers a different topic, so you can easily gain specific insights and have fun at the same time.

How To Study: Scientifically Proven Short Cuts to Better Grades in High School and College (New York, NY: Fawcett Premier, 1993), by Harry Maddox, is an older book that tackles study skills from a wide range of perspectives, including a student's motives, habits, health, and mental abilities. He supports his ideas with useful research, but beware that Maddox does not write from a Christian perspective. An added feature is a chapter that deals with group study and work. Overall, the insights you glean will be helpful. (This out-of-print title is available from <www.senecavalleybooks.com> or at your local library.)

The Elements of Style: 50th Anniversary Edition (Upper Saddle River, NJ: Longman Publishers, an imprint of Pearson Educational, 2008), by William Strunk, Jr., and E. B. White, is an enduring little volume that covers the basic rules of grammar and principles of composition that are most often violated. Questions in regard to form, words and expressions commonly mis-used, and style are covered as well. Strunk's direct, concise approach is both refreshing and beneficial. Two excellent companion volumes, *The Elements of Grammar* by Margaret Shertzer and *The Elements of Editing* by Arthur Plotnik, are also published by Macmillian—originally in 1986 and 1982, respectively.

APPENDIX III

NOVELS AND STORIES
YOU SHOULD READ

Good literature abounds in the English language, so all that could be listed cannot be held in such a small volume as this. Therefore, only a selected number of exceptional titles are mentioned here. For your own information, many agree that those who read the classics are better prepared for college and beyond. So for the best foundation possible, seek to develop a sound **reading program** now.

Fiction Books for Your Reading Pleasure

At the Back of the North Wind, by George MacDonald
Ben Hur, by Lew Wallace
Ivanhoe, by Sir Walter Scott
Last of the Mohicans, The, by James Fenimore Cooper
Little Women, by Louisa May Alcott

Narnia Chronicles, The, by C. S. Lewis
Northwest Passage, by Kenneth Roberts
Old Man and the Sea, The, by Ernest Hemingway
Oliver Twist, by Charles Dickens
Peterkin Papers, The, by Lucretia Hale

Rebecca of Sunnybrook Farm, by Kate Douglas Wiggins
Rip Van Winkle, by Washington Irving
Robinson Crusoe, by Daniel Defoe
Scottish Chiefs, by Jane Porter
Treasure Island, by Robert Louis Stevenson

Nonfiction Books for Your Reading Pantology

A Boy's War, by David Michell
Christianity and Liberalism, by J. G. Machen
Hiding Place, The, by Corrie ten Boom
John Bunyan, by Sandy Dengler

Mere Christianity, by C. S. Lewis
Microbe Hunters, by Paul De Kruif
Profiles in Courage, by John F. Kennedy
Story of My Life, by Helen Keller

There are numerous other selections that could have been mentioned; therefore, if you are searching for more titles, there are many bibliographies you may want to consult. The following resources may be found in your church's library, at your local Christian bookstore, or online—if not, ask someone to help you obtain them. For the younger reader, *Honey for a Child's Heart* (Zondervan, 2002), by Gladys Hunt, or *How to Grow a Young Reader: A Parent's Guide to Books for Kids* (Shaw Books, 1999), by Kathryn Lindskoog and Ranelda Mack Hunsicker, are both superb choices. A more exhaustive work called *Books Children Love: A Guide to the Best Children's Literature* (Crossway, 2002), by Elizabeth Laraway Wilson, contains over 300 pages of titles and brief snippets on each entry to help you further decide which one is right for you. *Books Children Love* also comes highly recommended. For high school students, *Honey for a Teen's Heart* (Zondervan, 2002), by Susan Hunt, will help your teen catch the reading habit and become a lover of good books. *The Book Tree: A Christian Reference for Children's Literature* (Canon Press, 2001), by Lizabeth McCallum and Jane Scott, is another wonderful resource that provides brief descriptions of numerous books ranging from the preschool level to the high school level and is available from Christian Liberty Press (visit <christianlibertypress.com> for more information). For the more advanced reader, check out *The Best Books: A Guide to Christian Literature*, by W. J. Grier (Banner of Truth Trust, 1968; now out of print but can be found on used-book websites).

And when all is said and done, remember the wisdom of King Solomon—"of making many books there is no end; and much study is a weariness of the flesh" (Ecclesiastes 12:12). God's best to you as you pursue your career as a student—"approved unto God."

To obtain a free catalog
describing the line of educational materials
that are offered by Christian Liberty Press, please contact:

Christian Liberty Press
502 W. Euclid Avenue
Arlington Heights, Illinois 60004
(800) 348-0899
www.christianlibertypress.com
www.shopChristianLiberty.com